**天涯论丛** 陈义华 ◎ 主编

# 黎族经典民间文学英译研究

马海燕 著

LIZU JINGDIAN MINJIAN WENXUE
YINGYI YANJIU

中山大学出版社

·广州·

版权所有　翻印必究

**图书在版编目（CIP）数据**

黎族经典民间文学英译研究/马海燕著. —广州：中山大学出版社，2022.12

（天涯论丛）

ISBN 978-7-306-07642-7

Ⅰ. ①黎… Ⅱ. ①马… Ⅲ. ①黎族—民间文学—英语—文学翻译—研究　Ⅳ. ①H315.9 ②I207.981

中国版本图书馆 CIP 数据核字（2022）第 206395 号

| | |
|---|---|
| 出 版 人： | 王天琪 |
| 策划编辑： | 嵇春霞 |
| 责任编辑： | 卢思敏 |
| 封面设计： | 曾　斌 |
| 责任校对： | 蓝若琪 |
| 责任技编： | 靳晓虹 |
| 出版发行： | 中山大学出版社 |
| 电　　话： | 编辑部 020-84113349，84111997，84110779，84110776 |
| | 发行部 020-84111998，84111981，84111160 |
| 地　　址： | 广州市新港西路 135 号 |
| 邮　　编： | 510275　　传　真：020-84036565 |
| 网　　址： | http://www.zsup.com.cn　E-mail: zdcbs@mail.sysu.edu.cn |
| 印 刷 者： | 佛山家联印刷有限公司 |
| 规　　格： | 787mm×1092mm　1/16　14.125 印张　193 千字 |
| 版次印次： | 2022 年 12 月第 1 版　2022 年 12 月第 1 次印刷 |
| 定　　价： | 52.00 元 |

如发现本书因印装质量影响阅读，请与出版社发行部联系调换

# 前　言

我国少数民族文学在中华民族文学中占有重要地位，而作为文学源头的民间创作，更是在我国少数民族文化史上占有特别重要的地位。各民族的神话、传说、故事、歌谣、谚语等，共同构成了璀璨夺目的民间文学宝库。海南黎族文学作为我国少数民族文学中的重要一支，以其旖旎多姿的形态吸引着广大读者。海南黎族文学大致可以划分为两个阶段：新中国成立之前，黎族文学主要是黎族人民口头创作的民间文学；新中国成立之后，海南逐渐涌现出黎族作家创作的书面文学。黎族民间文学由海南黎族人民在长期的生产和生活中口头创作并世代口口相传而来，反映了黎族人民对大自然的征服、对自然现象的理解以及对自身生活的讴歌，是人们了解黎族先民的活化石。目前，黎族民间故事已经被列入海南省级非物质文化遗产名录。

黎族民间文学经历了由自发形成到有组织地编纂的过程，目前，黎族民间文学已经形成一定的体系，亟待进行跨文化境外传播。对黎族民间文学进行梳理和翻译，研究其翻译过程中的策略和方法，对于传播黎族民间文学、讲好中国故事、树立民族文化自信具有非常重要的现实意义。本研究首先对黎族民间文学进行了概述，其次梳理了黎族民间文学的流变和发展，然后介绍了少数民族民间文学的翻译观，最后对黎族民间文学中的40个经典故事进行了英译，并解析了翻译过程中遇到的难点和处理的方法。

鉴于目前学界对黎族民间文学乃至少数民族民间文学的英译和研究都比较匮缺,本研究可作为少数民族民间文学英译研究的一次探索和尝试,旨在为该领域的研究抛砖引玉。书中如有谬误和不足之处,敬请方家批评指正!

本研究受到海南省哲学社会科学规划项目"新媒体时代海南特色非遗文化传播模式研究[项目号:HNSK(YB)22-107]"支持,特此感谢!

# 目 录

## 第一章　黎族民间文学概述 …………………………… 1
　一、黎族民间文学的形成 …………………………… 2
　二、黎族民间文学的研究 …………………………… 3
　三、黎族民间文学的分类 …………………………… 4

## 第二章　黎族民间文学的流变与发展 ………………… 9
　一、黎族民间神话与汉族神话之间的关系 …………… 10
　　1. 开天辟地神话 ………………………………… 10
　　2. 人类起源神话 ………………………………… 11
　二、黎族神话中"雷公"形象的流变 ………………… 11
　三、黎族民间文学中的作家再创作 …………………… 13
　四、黎族民间文学的价值 …………………………… 14

## 第三章　黎族经典民间文学的英译 …………………… 17
　一、黎族民间文学英译的重要性 ……………………… 18
　二、少数民族民间文学的翻译观 ……………………… 18
　　1. 文化的翻译观 ………………………………… 18
　　2. 政治的翻译观 ………………………………… 19
　　3. 归化、异化翻译观 …………………………… 20
　　4. 保留原味的翻译观 …………………………… 22
　三、黎族民间文学中经典的选取和翻译 ……………… 24
　　1. 原文的选取原则 ……………………………… 24
　　2. 翻译策略的选择 ……………………………… 25

**第四章　黎族民间故事译例解析** …… 27
　一、专名和通名的区分和翻译 …… 28
　　1．"雷公"的译法 …… 28
　　2．"黎"的译法 …… 29
　　3．"黎母"的译法 …… 30
　　4．"山神"的译法 …… 30
　　5．"大力神"的译法 …… 30
　二、文化特色词的英译 …… 31
　　1．"俚人"的译法 …… 31
　　2．"村峒"的译法 …… 31
　　3．"黄道婆"的译法 …… 32
　三、词语的使用与人物形象的塑造问题 …… 32
　四、流水句的翻译策略 …… 33
　五、情歌的翻译 …… 34
　　1．对称谓进行变译 …… 35
　　2．对喻体进行变译 …… 35
　　3．尽量做到押韵 …… 35

**第五章　黎族经典民间故事汉英对照** …… 37
　故事一　人类的起源 …… 38
　故事二　黎母的神话 …… 42
　故事三　万家——关于山区和平原的传说 …… 45
　故事四　伟代造动物 …… 47
　故事五　大力神 …… 50
　故事六　雷公根 …… 53
　故事七　兄弟星座 …… 57
　故事八　三套神衣 …… 62
　故事九　陵水县县名的由来 …… 67

故事十　马伏波与白马井 …………………………… 69

故事十一　冼夫人解救俚女 …………………………… 71

故事十二　纺织女神黄道婆 …………………………… 75

故事十三　五指山的传说 ……………………………… 79

故事十四　七仙岭 ……………………………………… 83

故事十五　鹿回头村 …………………………………… 90

故事十六　落笔洞 ……………………………………… 95

故事十七　亚龙湾 ……………………………………… 102

故事十八　万泉河 ……………………………………… 104

故事十九　天涯湾与南天一柱 ………………………… 106

故事二十　甘工鸟 ……………………………………… 108

故事二十一　椰子的由来 ……………………………… 111

故事二十二　黎族三月三节 …………………………… 113

故事二十三　纹面的传说 ……………………………… 116

故事二十四　鼻箫 ……………………………………… 122

故事二十五　黎族蜡染的来历 ………………………… 124

故事二十六　黎族倒挂树枝、撒灶灰的习俗 ………… 126

故事二十七　望夫石 …………………………………… 130

故事二十八　兄弟俩 …………………………………… 134

故事二十九　色开成家 ………………………………… 139

故事三十　龟女婿 ……………………………………… 144

故事三十一　红蘑菇与白蘑菇 ………………………… 151

故事三十二　阿勇智斗山神 …………………………… 156

故事三十三　百兽衣 …………………………………… 160

故事三十四　聪明的媳妇 ……………………………… 168

故事三十五　水与火的故事 …………………………… 174

故事三十六　哥喂鸟 …………………………………… 176

故事三十七　捉弄财主 ………………………………… 180

故事三十八　继母 …………………………………………… 185

故事三十九　藤桥救妹 ………………………………………… 189

故事四十　老课将军 …………………………………………… 201

**参考文献** ……………………………………………………… 215

# 第一章 黎族民间文学概述

## 一、黎族民间文学的形成

黎族是最早居住在海南岛的少数民族。根据史料记载和考古发现，黎族被认为是中国南方古代越族中的一支——骆越，在约3000年前陆续从南方沿海大陆迁移到海南岛，并在长期的历史发展过程中吸收了其他民族成分（主要是汉族）而逐渐形成并发展起来（刘耀荃，1986）。史图博（1964）从人种学和民族志的视角考察发现，黎族的部分支系可能来自东南亚国家。

黎族社会经历了一个相当漫长的无阶级社会时期，在这一时期没有统治者，人们之间没有利害冲突，唯一的"敌人"就是大自然。因此，黎族文学在萌芽阶段反映的就是人与自然争斗的内容。他们通过丰富的想象力和创造力，创作出一系列远古神话和传说。在这些神话和传说中，我们可以了解黎族的起源和洪荒时代中那些理想化的英雄人物及其英雄事迹，如洪水的传说、大力神的故事等。此外，当时还出现了一些反映美好道德观念的故事。这就是黎族先民在远古时期给我们带来的照进口头文学的曙光。社会始终在发展，随着生产力的进步，黎族社会进入了阶级社会。私有制产生的同时也伴随着阶级矛盾的产生，表现在口头文学上，就是题材更加广泛，很多神话和民间故事中既有对坚贞爱情的颂扬，也有对人民辛勤智慧的褒赞，同时还有对统治阶级丑恶嘴脸的揭露和对人民悲惨生活的慨叹。这时，口头文学中的民歌和民谣占据主流。黎族传统民歌的内容包括生活、劳作、爱情、祭祀、婚姻和摇篮曲等，各种题材的民谣的表现形式也不同，比如，生活歌谣的基调哀怨低沉，劳动歌谣的曲调昂扬有激情。

黎族文学深受黎族传统文化的影响，这在文学作品中得到了充分体现。首先，黎族文学深受黎族传统美德的影响。黎族传统美德世代相传，长久以来成为黎族百姓的生活理念和行为准则。体现在作品中的黎族传统美德就有吃苦耐劳、对正义的歌颂和弘扬、对恶势力的鞭挞和惩戒等。其次，黎族文学也深受黎族传统信仰的影响。"黎族文化中的重要组成就是其传统信仰，黎族人民具有独特的本民族宗教信仰。黎族民族信仰的核心是——万物有灵。"[①] 从前，在黎族人民心中，只要是有灵性的自然物都会作祟于人们，导致人生病。为了躲避灾祸，人就要对这些自然物敬仰膜拜。这些传统的民间信仰已经渗入黎族人民的生活中，其言行举止都流露出对鬼神的崇拜。（曲明鑫，2015）

## 二、黎族民间文学的研究

现有对黎族民间文学的研究主要从民间文学作品的搜集和整理、理论研究两方面展开，涉及黎族民歌、神话故事等内容。韩伯泉、郭小东的《黎族民间文学概说》是出版得较早的一部专著，该书从黎族传统歌谣、神话传说、革命歌谣、民间叙事长诗、谜语与谚语、民间歌手等几个方面展开分析论述。这部专著虽未正式出版，但在黎族民间文学研究领域却有一定的影响。

由于黎族没有本民族的文字，黎族民间文学在历史上只能以口头形式代代传递。其因种类多样，内容丰富，在黎族文学中占有极为重要的位置。在民间文学作品搜集和整理方面，现已公开出版多部作品。保亭黎族苗族自治县、白沙黎族自治县等民族自治县的文化部门组织编印了不少有关黎族民间故事、歌谣、民间谚语和谜语等的文献资料。1984年，中华人民共和国文化部[②]、中华人民共和国国家民族事务委员会、中国民间文艺研究会[③]联合启动了在全国范围内编辑出版中国民间文学"三套集成"的浩大工程，其中的海南各卷搜集了大量各类黎族民间文学作品；比较全面的黎族民间文

---

① 国家民族事务委员会全国少数民族古籍整理研究室：《中国少数民族古籍总目提要：黎族卷》，中国大百科全书出版社2010年版。
② 今中华人民共和国文化和旅游部。
③ 今中国民间文艺家协会。

学作品集还有符桂花主编的《黎族民间故事大集》《黎族传统民歌三千首》。此外，具有一定影响力的著作还有王文华搜集和整理的民间叙事长诗《甘工鸟》。王文华于20世纪90年代初，利用自身谙熟本民族生活和语言的优势，长期在黎族村庄蹲点，采录并整理出完整的民间叙事长诗《甘工鸟》《猎歌与仙妹》，将两首民间叙事长诗结成专集，以《甘工鸟》为书名出版。张跃虎搜集和整理的传统黎歌集《五指山风》共收录了111首汉译传统黎歌。与《甘工鸟》一样，这本集子的难能可贵之处也在于作者在搜集和整理时尽可能地保留了"原汁原味"。王月圣的《黎族创世歌》分为颂歌、生产歌、风情歌、苦闷歌、快乐歌、相逢相送歌、猜对歌和旅游歌等九个部分，记录了乐东黎族自治县的黎族民歌唱词，是真实反映当地民族风情的口述整理材料。另外还有卓其德的《美满的歌》《浪花》等。这些研究成果多为学者深入民间收集记录和归纳整理而成，重民族志记述，深入分析较少。

在民间文学理论研究方面，韩伯泉和郭小东合著的《黎族民间文学概说》是最早的一部系统研究黎族民间文学的专著，该专著在黎族民间文学研究领域具有较为广泛的影响。陈立浩、范高庆、苏鹏程合著的《黎族文学概览》上编对黎族民间文学设专章或专节论述。王海、江冰合著的《从远古走向现代——黎族文化与黎族文学》一书也谈到黎族民间文学，由于该书拥有大量第一手资料，其论述更具真实性和可靠性。除此之外，还有不少单篇研究文章在各种刊物上发表。从对黎族民间文学研究的文献资料来看，黎族民间文学作品和有关黎族民间文学的研究著作、文章比较丰富。

## 三、黎族民间文学的分类

黎族民间文学内容丰富，形式多样，包含神话、传说、故事、歌谣、叙事长诗、谜语和谚语等多种体裁。

神话是民间文学的源头之一，王海在其于2009年发表的论文

《黎族神话类型略论》中将黎族神话分为开辟神话、人类起源（族源）神话、洪水神话、自然神话和英雄神话五种类型。他还分析了黎族民间故事中所蕴含的传统道德精神及其与黎族社会生活的密切联系。（向丽，2013）

黎族神话的内容十分广泛，涉及开天辟地、人类起源、人神相争等多个方面。在黎族神话传说中，关于黎族的起源有多种解释，其中也包含女始祖方面的内容，比较典型的是《纳加西拉鸟》。故事的大致内容是，黎族的祖先有个女儿，出生后不久母亲就去世了，被一只名为"纳加西拉"的鸟口含谷类哺育长大。为了不忘鸟的养育之恩，以后的黎族妇女便一代传一代地在身体文上"纳加西拉"鸟翅膀的花纹，以志纪念。该故事解释了黎族的族源，也解释了黎族妇女文身习俗的起源。这毫无疑问是图腾崇拜的表现，同时也明显地反映了母系氏族社会的特征。这类有关女始祖的神话传说，较有代表性的还有《黎母山传说》。其他具有代表性的神话作品有描述世界形成的《大力神》、展现人类与自然的关系的《雷公根》等。

黎族的民间传说种类则更为多样，代表作有反映农事活动和历史事件的《台风的传说》，描述黎乡独有风物、风貌特征的传说《五指山的传说》《七指岭的传说》《鹿回头》等，记载人物和史事的传说《英雄花》《黄道婆的故事》《李德裕的传说》等，讲述黎族人传统生活习俗的《三月三的传说》，传递多重含义的动植物传说《牛为什么犁地》《山兰稻种》等。

民间故事是一种特点异常突出、极具艺术魅力的传统故事。它突出的特点之一，就是有很强的幻想性，而这种幻想性又是根植于民间丰饶的现实生活土壤的。在神奇故事中，以爱情为题材的作品为数不少，类型也很多。例如，在汉族和一些兄弟民族中，都广泛流传着神魔参与人间生活，与凡人结为夫妻的故事，其中包括龙王公主、田螺姑娘、牡丹仙子、狐狸媳妇、鹿姑娘等与穷小子喜结良缘者，也包括蛇郎、冬瓜儿、青蛙骑手等娶百姓姑娘为妻者。这类故事往往通过幻想的形式，使自然界中的物和景、社会生活中的人和事变形，富有奇幻的色彩地表现出人们的理想、愿望和对美好爱情的憧憬。（王海，2005）黎族的民间故事不仅展现了黎族人民的现实生活，还传达着黎族人民丰富的思想感情。黎族民间故事中的代表作品有《星娘》《阿坚治黎头》《一个瞎子、一个跛子和一个驼子》《兄弟俩》《槟榔的故事》《椰子壳》《老树和乌鸦》《水族舞会》等。（黄欣，2014）

丰富的歌谣也是黎族民间文学的重要组成部分。早在渔猎生活时代，黎族已出现有原始劳动号子味道的短歌，以及吟唱鸟兽虫鱼习性特征的《禽兽谣》。在数千年的历史长河中，黎族人民在生产和生活中创作出了内容丰富、地域有别、曲调各异的民歌，如砍山伐木歌《呼嘿调》、摇篮催眠歌《呵唎调》、斗牛歌《叽呃调》、白沙民歌《哇呀哇调》、乐东民歌《千家调》、叙事长诗《婚歌》和《巴定》等。（陈立浩等，2008）黎族民歌的格律大概是这样的：关于黎歌每节的行数，在与汉族杂居或接近汉族的地区，用海南汉语唱的，常常是四句一节（也有八句的）。古典黎歌中有一种短小精练的"四情歌"，也是四句的。此外，大多数黎族民歌每节没有固定的行数，从两三行到十行以上，没有限制。黎歌句子最常见的两种是五言和七言，也有以五言、七言为主体，其中掺入一些三言以至十言以上长短不等的句子。短歌一般是整齐的五言、七言，较长的叙事民歌则采用长短不等的句子。黎歌很讲究节奏韵律，音乐性很强，音韵和谐，容易上口；加上语言凝练，又富口语化，通俗易懂，便于背诵。黎族民歌一般的规律是这样的：开头第一行的最后一个韵与第二行中任何一个韵都可以协韵；第二行的最后一个韵又都可以与第三行中的任何一个韵协韵；这样一直到最后一行，连锁地协韵，十分灵活。黎歌的表现方法和语言运用也很讲究。许多流传久远的黎歌都善于运用黎族人民所熟悉的事物，具体而形象地表情达意，而且常常大胆地使用一连串生动贴切的比喻，丰富多彩，引起人们丰富的想象，把人们引入新奇和美妙的意境。

## 第一章
### 黎族民间文学概述

  黎族的叙事长诗主要包括黎族创世、人类起源、歌颂爱情、不屈抗争四个主题。黎族代表性的创世史诗是《五指山传》。这部已正式出版的长诗长达3000余行，规模宏大，以连贯的情节对黎族的起源和黎族先祖的创世经历进行了全面的描述，被认为是黎族人民的一部百科全书。反映人类起源方面的作品主要有《姐弟俩》《阿丢和阿藤的故事》，都讲述了在父亲受蒙骗的情形下，遭后母虐待的姐弟俩被迫来到荒无人烟的深山老林，在鸟兽、仙人的帮助下顽强地生存下来，并遵雷公的旨意结为夫妻，繁衍了黎族子孙后代的故事。歌颂爱情方面的代表作有《甘工鸟》和《猎哥与仙妹》。《甘工鸟》讲述了勤劳勇敢、聪明美丽的黎族姑娘甘娲不堪忍受父母兄长的逼婚，偷偷将身上的银项圈舂成双翅，从夫家化鸟而去的故事。《猎哥与仙妹》讲述了男女主人公不畏强权，对爱情忠贞不渝，为实现美好的愿望，面对恶势力的阻挠奋起反抗，最后惩治了邪恶，获得了幸福的故事。表现斗争主题的作品有叙事诗《龙蓬》（原名《不嫁歌》）等。该诗以一个女孩子不愿意嫁给名叫"亚龙"的"龙公"为引子，通过对劳动场景和日常生活情形的描绘，展示了黎族合亩制①中的人际关系，表达了"龙仔"们对为人自私、苛刻的"龙公"的憎恨厌恶，反映了在黎族合亩共耕经济末期剥削者与劳动者之间的对立、矛盾和斗争的社会现实。（王海，2005）

  黎族民间谚语也是黎族人民在长期的生产生活中创造出来的，反映的内容有自然现象、对四季的观察、对农事活动的总结，以及人与人之间的相处之道等。黎族为百越之后裔，而古代百越民族成功地改良了野生稻，很早就开始了水稻农业生产。因此，黎族人民重视自然生态的变化，对天上的云彩星月，以及地上的物候、地象等，都十分用心观察，创造出大量关于星象与天气的谚语，例如：

---

  ① 中华人民共和国成立前海南岛部分黎族地区特有的一种生产和社会组织。"合亩"一词在黎语中意为"大伙做工"。"龙仔"是因贫穷或受迫害而投靠他人的人，"龙公"则是被投靠者，绝大多数为亩头。部分亩头往往由于占有较多的生产资料，利用自己的地位和某些特权，在分配中多得产品，对"龙仔"进行各种剥削。

"夜里星光明,来日天气晴";"今晚满天星,明日大晴天";"星成团,地成潭";"天星疏,地下枯";"天星密,地上湿";"星星眨眼,下雨不远";等等。此外,还有反映人际关系,讲求做人道理方面的谚语,例如:"钱财不要紧,真理最值钱";"轻重用秤称,是非用理评";"马服鞭子,人服道理";等等。(陈兰,2012)

# 第二章

## 黎族民间文学的流变与发展

## 一、黎族民间神话与汉族神话之间的关系

### 1. 开天辟地神话

各民族创作的开天辟地神话,与他们所处时代的地域特征、生产劳动和原始信仰密不可分。茅盾(1981)先生在《神话杂论》一文中指出:"即凡落后民族的开辟神话大概是极简陋的,渐高则渐复杂,至于文明民族,则开辟神话大都是极复杂,含有解释自然的用意,富于文学气味,并且自成系统。"但是黎族的创世神话《大力神的传说》却不简陋,该神话内容精彩、叙事完整、内涵丰富、意蕴深刻,既有开天辟地的内容,又有日月神话的内容,可谓内容丰富精彩。黎族的原始先民认为天地最初"相距只有几丈①远",是大力神这位开天辟地的巨人,"把身躯伸高一万丈,把天空拱高一万丈",这样天地才生成。这与汉族神话《盘古》中的盘古开天辟地有相似之处。三国时吴国人徐整的《三五历纪》中对盘古开天辟地的神话如此记载:"天地混沌如鸡子,盘古生其中⋯⋯一日九变,神于天,圣于地,天日高一丈,地日厚一丈。如此万八千岁,天数极高,地数极深,盘古极长。"两者有所不同的是,黎族神话里面大力神拱高天地之时,人类已经存在,而盘古开天辟地之时天地一片混沌,还没有人类出现。《大力神》中关于日月的神话与汉族神话《后羿射日》又有异曲同工之妙:相同之处是天上都出现了多个太阳和月亮,人们无法生存,神来解决人类的烦恼,所用武器都是弓箭;不同之处在于,《大力神》这则黎族神话中是七个太阳和七个月亮,而汉族神话中是十个太阳。据《淮南子·本经训》记载:"尧之时,十日并出,焦禾稼,杀草木,而民无所食。"

可见,黎族民间神话与汉族民间神话之间既有相同的母本来

---

① 1丈≈3.33米。

源,又有其独特之处,这是由黎族人本身来源的特殊性决定的。他们本是古代百越民族的一个分支,但由于长期独居孤岛,与大陆隔绝,因此在保留相同母本的基础上,其民间神话又有了不同的生发。

### 2. 人类起源神话

各民族都有关于人类起源的神话,这是人类对自身起源的思考和探索。在黎族人聚居的不同区域也流传着不同的神话,如流传在五指山区的《南瓜的故事》,开篇有歌唱道:"盘古开天造人世,人类分排男与女。老当老定两兄弟,南瓜开花育男女。天灾地祸毁万类,南瓜肚内存后裔。老先荷发造人纪,传下三族创天地。"这说的是"南瓜开花育男女"的故事。此外,具有代表性的还有《黎母山传说》。在这个故事中,雷公放了一颗蛇卵在高山中,后来他击破蛇卵,蛇卵里面跳出一个女孩子,雷公为其起名叫黎母。黎母长大后与一个从大陆渡海过来采沉香的男子结婚,繁衍了黎族的子孙。

从这两则流传在黎族人聚居的不同区域的神话可以看出,黎族的人类起源说受到了汉族人类起源神话的影响。《南瓜的故事》一开头说的也是盘古开天造人世,这与汉族的盘古开天辟地是一样的,后来才有南瓜开花育人,再后来人世间经历了毁灭性的灾难,人躲在南瓜肚里才得以存活下来,繁衍后代。而在《黎母山传说》中,黎母是由雷公用蛇卵孕育出来的,但是男子却是从大陆渡海来海南岛的,这一方面体现出黎族原始先民对蛇的图腾信仰,另一方面反映出黎族原始先民与大陆之间的联系,也从侧面印证了黎族原始先民有可能是从大陆迁徙到海南岛的。

## 二、黎族神话中"雷公"形象的流变

"雷公"是黎族民间文学作品中常见的形象,在黎族先民生活中占据着非常重要的地位,这与黎族先民的居住环境和气候条件密切相关。黎族先民居住在偏僻的海岛上,与大陆文化隔绝,他们在与恶劣的自然环境斗争的过程中,先是由于自身的羸弱而对大自然心存敬畏,后来逐渐学会了利用工具尤其是火,自身的生存能力增强,于是对大自然产生了一种抗争的心理。海南岛地处热带地区,热带风暴非常常见,电闪雷鸣是黎族原始先民无法抵抗而又心存敬畏和恐惧的自然现象,因此也成了黎族原始先民想象最多的意象。黎族先民怕雷公,认为大小灾难都是源于触犯了"雷公鬼",而反映在黎族神话中,就是雷公形象的多次改变。

在早期的人类起源神话中,雷公具有法力无边、心地善良、为民服务的正面形象。例如,《黎母山传说》中的雷公是人类的缔造者,是人们敬仰的创世神;在《人类的起源》《洪水传说》《葫芦瓜》《螃蟹精》《南瓜的故事》等神话中,劫后余生的兄妹无一不是遵循了神明雷公的旨意而婚配,承担起繁衍人类的重任;与洪水遗民型神话相近的人类起源传说《姐弟俩》,也述说了姐弟俩遵雷公旨意婚配而繁衍后人的故事。

但到了后来,雷公的形象从受人敬仰变得令人类失望,甚至作为破坏人们幸福的帮凶出现。例如,《螃蟹的传说》里,为惩治一只肆虐人间的巨蟹,人类请来了他们认为无所不能的雷公为民除害。然而,雷公来势虽猛,最终却败阵而去。后来,人类又请来了雨神、风神,才彻底制服了巨蟹。这时的雷公在人们心目中的神威无疑已经大减。在带有神话色彩的神奇故事《阿德哥和七仙妹》里,玉帝欲拆散真心相爱的阿德与七仙妹,七仙妹誓死不从,雷公奉命手执巨斧劈断五指山与天庭之间的通途,使七仙妹与其他六位仙姐从此天地相隔。地方传说《双女石》中的两位仙女同情凡人生活的艰难,每天都悄悄来到南海为民造福。雷公和电母奉王母娘娘之命捉拿两位仙女不成,于是,雷公淫威大发,将仙女们并肩化成的双峰石轰然炸开,使其裂成了三块。这两则故事里的雷公则成了一个助纣为虐的极其可憎的神。

再后来,雷公的形象更是沦落到与人为敌、受人追杀的地步。例如,在黎族神话《雷公根》中,雷公一开始是黎族青年打占的朋友,后来因恐吓百姓、偷盗打占的豹尾和藤条而受到打占的追杀,被砍掉左脚并煮熟,后被弃置在地上,变成了一种植物"雷公根"。神话中的雷公形象已经变成人类的对手,而且是失败的对手。作为一种象征,故事中的胜利者打占是远古黎族人民征服自然的愿望、勇气和力量的体现,是人为万物之灵和宇宙主宰的思想主题的生动表达。同样在《雷公为什么在天上叫》中,居心不良的雷公欲祸害人间,却被人间本领超凡的三兄弟砍伤了脚,每逢下雨浸到伤口便剧痛难忍,发出震天动地的叫喊。该神话也解释了打雷这一自然现象的由来。

从雷公形象的变化可以看出黎族人对大自然的认识经历了从蒙昧的害怕,到尝试认识并进行对抗,最后试图征服大自然的漫长过程。

## 三、黎族民间文学中的作家再创作

正因为黎族民间文学是从黎族人民的劳动和斗争中产生和成长起来,又在劳动和斗争中不断得到丰富和发展的,所以它有着强大的生命力。但是,由于黎族一直处在生产力发展水平落后的社会阶段,特别是没有自己的文字,其民间文学长期靠口头创作、口头传唱,不易得到完整保留。有时,一个故事有头有尾,甚至在传唱的过程中越来越丰富完整,但是口传久远,因为老一代人亡物故,又难免会有遗漏,或者出现张冠李戴的情况,甚至有失传的危险。

一些作家和民俗学家在黎族民间采风的过程中,为了使原先口头传唱的黎族民间故事或民歌等的内容更加完整、丰富,表达形式和语言更具有吸引力,在采风和转录的过程中,增加了个人的创作成分。例如,杜桐(1960)在20世纪50年代末于海南黎族苗族自治州工作期间,经常下乡实地考察采风,发现黎族几位传唱者对黎族民歌《甘工鸟》的传承不完整。此外，原先传唱的内容是阿甘的后母为了钱财和牛羊把阿甘许配给财主帕三顺，阿甘的哥哥虽然同情阿甘，不想让她变作鸟，但是实际上却骗阿甘，要把她抓住，最后，阿甘拼命逃脱，变成鸟而得以自由飞走。杜桐"为了提高和加强故事主题思想的人民性，丰富故事的内容和情节又能保存原来故事的基本轮廓，做到在原来的基础上提高"，故而采取了"取其精华，去其糟粕"的原则。原故事之所以动人，在于它表现了阿甘为了争取自由幸福的婚姻，坚强反抗压迫，宁为飞鸟，不甘屈辱。杜桐认为这是故事的精华之所在。但原故事把压迫者指认为后母，放过了罪魁祸首帕三顺，是本末倒置，严重地削弱了故事的思想性。杜桐把压迫者指认为峒主，把阿甘父母写成良善的爹娘，将同情阿甘和劳海的人扩大到广泛的村邻、峒民和远在海滨的渔翁，而不仅止于阿甘的哥哥、妹妹和嫂嫂。

这种对原口头创作的更改一方面基于作者对文学作品主题意义的理解，另一方面也有时代背景的影响。杜桐创作的年代是20世纪50年代末，当时中国的社会环境强调阶级斗争和反抗地主阶级的压迫，文学的主题自然也如此。

## 四、黎族民间文学的价值

黎族民间文学具有重要的价值。以传说为例，首先，可以增强民族凝聚力。传说是一个社会群体对某一历史事件或历史人物的公共记忆，属于特定聚落空间内部的共同记忆，而地方传说将族群记忆添附在特定的山岳峰峦、江河湖泊里，对身边的这些山水景观赋予历史内涵和文化内涵，构筑本族群的民间历史和共同的社会记忆，形成族群内部的族群认同和文化认同，从而使山水传说具有了热爱乡土、增进团结、促进和谐的社会功能。祖先的历史并不强调所谓"客观与真实"，重要的是它形成了源远流长的社会记忆。在族群内部成员的意识中，记忆共存的历史是值得崇敬和可信的，一代又一代深深地镌刻在族群每一个成员的脑海中,族群成员在对祖先的共同追忆中延续着对族群的认同。其实,我们研究传说并不是要探索过去的事实,而是先人为何要以口头文学的形式来保存某种记忆,即对他们的真实意图进行探索。在这个意义上,传说也可以被看作一部关于民众日常生产生活知识的生动的口头教科书。

其次,可以增加人们对地方景观的美学意识。民间传说中关于地名的故事通常以自然和人文景观为中心,运用夸张、渲染、幻想、变形等手法,通过生动的形象和传奇的情节令自然美上升为艺术美,给民众以审美享受。例如,关于五指山、七指岭的传说,都在故事的叙述中凸显了山的形状和特征,游客结合相关传说游历景点时,能留有更深的印象;而黎族地方传说大部分都是完整的故事,有相对完整的情节、生动的人物形象以及充满趣味性的叙述,这些能引导人们在脑海中勾勒出传说文本和山水景物"和谐统一"的画面。

最后,可以提升地方文化的旅游价值。旅游文化资源包括以文物、史迹、遗址、古建筑为代表的古文化,以现代文化、艺术、科学、技术成果为代表的新文化,以日常生活习俗、节日庆典、口头文学、体育活动和服饰为代表的民俗文化和以人际交流为代表的伦理文化。地方传说属于民俗旅游资源中口头文学艺术的范畴,特别是那些具有完整人物、事件、场景等故事性元素的传说文本,它们为民俗文化旅游提供了具体有效的文学载体。在许多情况下,地方传说还是直接的旅游产品,往往体现在导游词或旅游文化读本等形式之中。而较为经典的地方传说,如"鹿回头"和"落笔洞",已经被海南省三亚市的大型歌舞展演《三亚千古情》收录,其中抽象化的口头或书面形式民间传说被转化为实物化的静态展示和形象化的旅游表演,已成为综合反映地方民俗文化的旅游产品。(黄晓坚,2019)

# 第三章

## 黎族经典民间文学的英译

## 一、黎族民间文学英译的重要性

在全球一体化不断深化的 21 世纪，全世界各个国家、各个民族之间的交流不断加深。这种互通不仅仅是经济上和政治上的，更是文化上的。我国作为有着 5000 年悠久历史的文化大国，有必要讲好本国故事，而要讲好本国故事，就必须深入挖掘我国 56 个民族的优质传统文化，并坚持"取其精华，去其糟粕"的原则，输出能弘扬中华民族优良品德，与当今时代主旋律相契合的正能量文化。黎族作为我国少数民族之一，其悠久的历史和一代又一代人对文化的薪火相传使其拥有了丰富的文化积淀，而黎族民间文学更是这丰厚的文化遗产中的瑰宝。民族的就是世界的，要让世界更好地接受黎族民间文学，就需要我们做好翻译工作。英语是国际通用语言，黎族民间文学的英译就成为一项必需的工作。

## 二、少数民族民间文学的翻译观

### 1. 文化的翻译观

翻译根植于语言所处的文化背景，绝对不是一个纯粹的语言行为。巴斯奈特（Susan Bassnett，1945—）的著作《翻译研究》（*Translation Studies*）对文化翻译观的基本内涵有如下解释：第一，翻译研究要以文化为基本的单位，而不单单停留在语言层面。第二，翻译不是简单的译码—重组过程，更是一种交流的行为，包括文化内部和文化之间的相互交流。语言和文化的关系十分密切，语言是文化的重要组成部分，同时又是文化的载体。通过语言，人们得以了解各个民族的习俗、思维特点和生活方式，文化深深地扎根于语言之中。因此，译者必须是一个真正意义上的文化人，在了解本民族文化的同时，也要了解外国文化，洞察两者的异同之处。第三，翻译不是简单描述原语文本，而是寻求该文本在另一种文化中的功能等值。翻译应该是一个动态的转换过程，在需要达成功能上的一致时，译者必须对原文进行相应的调整。也就是说，译者在两种文化差异较大时有权利根据需要对原文进行增减修改，以达到更好地传达原文文化内涵的目的，更好地实现文化意义上的功能等值。第四，由于文化群体有不同的需要，在不同的历史时期，翻译的原则和规范可以有所不同，翻译的目的就是满足不同文化群体的需要。（刘唱、闫一亮、徐思鹏，2020）

在译介过程中，译者不能只从字面上将这些故事转换为目的语即英语，还应充分传达其背后蕴含的中国文化，考虑中国传统文化与英语语言文化的异同，有意识地发扬特定的文化知识，促进跨文化交际。翻译时不必机械拘泥于某一固定形式，可以灵活采取直译、意译、加注等方法，最大限度地传达文化信息，促进辉煌的民间文学走向世界。（魏怡，2015）

## 2. 政治的翻译观

潘文国教授在为《翻译与冲突——叙事性阐释》（*Translation and Conflict: A Narrative Account*）中文版所作的序言中指出：翻译研究的文化转向使翻译研究的重心从原文转向了译文，从"忠实于原著"转向关注译文的社会功能。但是文化派的多数研究仍停留在翻译的文化功能上。而莫娜·贝克（Mona Baker，1953—）的翻译叙事理论比前人又进了一步，认为翻译本身就是政治的一部分，而且翻译还创造政治。不论在笔译场合还是口译场合，翻译都是国际政治斗争的一个组成部分。谢天振教授的序言也持类似的观点：翻译并不是简单的两种文字的转换，它不是在真空中进行的，作为不同语言、文字、民族之间的文学、文化交流行为，它必然还是一种受制于意识形态、赞助人、诗学观念等诸多因素的政治行为。（郭彧斌，2020）

## 3. 归化、异化翻译观

语言是文化的载体，文化与语言相互关联，密不可分，民族文学翻译必然涉及源语和译入语的文化背景，故归化和异化的区分实际上是文学翻译中文化策略的选择问题。归化（domestication）指在文学翻译中恪守本族文化的语言文化传统，回归地道的本族语表达方式。相反，异化（foreignization）指在翻译策略上迁就原作中的语言文化特点，采用倾向于外来语的表达方式。与归化和异化问题直接相关的就是语言处理层面的直译与意译的问题。

最早提出归化、异化概念的是德国神学家和翻译学家施莱尔马赫（Friedrich Daniel Ernst Schleiermacher，1768—1834）。早在其于1813年发表的一篇论文中，他就指出："译员要么尽量不去打扰作者，让读者向作者靠拢；要么尽量不要去打扰读者，让作者尽量向读者靠拢。"

但施莱尔马赫并未对二者在翻译实践中的应用展开论述。当代翻译学中明确提出归化、异化理论的是意大利裔美国学者韦努蒂（Lawrence Venuti，1953—），他于1995年在《译者的隐身》（*The Translator's Invisibility*）中写道："一是归化法，用民族中心主义强行使外国文本符合译入语的文化价值，把原作者带入译语文化；一是异化法，用非种族主义将外国文本的语言文化特征强加于译入语的文化价值，将读者带入外国情境。"

选择归化或异化对广泛涉及文化内涵的文学翻译而言，一直是个重要议题。在西方，勒弗维尔（André Lefevere，1946—1996）主张归化的翻译策略，认为异化译法的译文对译入语读者来说怪异难懂。奈达（Eugene Albert Nida，1914—2011）提出将译文的表达模式纳入译文读者的文化范畴，也更倾向于归化译法。但韦努蒂（Lawrence Venuti，1953—）从文学、文化和政治的高度建议采用异化翻译。他认为归化法是一种民族中心主义、种族主义、文化自恋和帝国主义的体现，是一种文化干预战略。

## 第三章
### 黎族经典民间文学的英译

我国翻译界对归化和异化的争论也由来已久。我国现代文学翻译初期基本以归化为主调，尤其是19世纪末至20世纪初的头10年。这主要是由当时的国情造成的。当时的中国与外界交流极少，民族危机空前深重，文学成为改良社会、教育民众的工具。过多的异化会阻碍译本思想的传播。五四运动后的十几年里，以鲁迅和瞿秋白为代表的"忠实派"译者有意识地采取异化的译法，以期从外国文学中吸取营养，达到改造文学、改造社会的目的，但同时也导致了一定程度上的生硬翻译。因此，其后归化法又占据了主导地位，傅雷的"神似说"以及钱钟书的"化境论"都是后来归化法的代表理论。显然，归化和异化在中国的翻译史上是交替出现的。近年来，这场争论再次变得激烈，越来越多的翻译工作者认识到在国际合作和交流日益加强的情况下，异化策略有助于保持异国风味和情调，从而开阔译文读者的眼界、提高其对异质文化的包容能力，进而丰富译入语的语言和文化。

与归化和异化之争相联系的是直译与意译之争。一般认为，译文的形式与内容都与原作贴近谓之直译；内容一致而形式不同谓之意译，即以原作意义为标准，在译文表达形式上另辟蹊径。需要指出的是，归化和异化不同于直译与意译。王东风教授在《归化与异化：矛与盾的交锋?》一文中对两者做了比较深入的探讨：

> 归化和异化可看作直译和意译的概念延伸，但并不完全等同于直译与意译。……如果说直译和意译是语言层次的讨论，那么归化和异化则是将语言层次的讨论延续升格至文化、诗学和政治层面。也就是说，直译和意译之争的靶心是意义和形式的得失问题，而归化和异化之争的靶心则是处在意义和形式得失旋涡中的文化身份、文学性乃至话语权力的得失问题。[①]

---

[①] 王东风：《归化与异化：矛与盾的交锋?》，载《中国翻译》2002年第5期，第24-26页。

可见，归化和异化是文学翻译中的文化策略问题，而直译与意译则是语言策略问题。二者虽然都是关于文学翻译中的语言文化立场选择的问题，但前者是宏观的立场和策略，而后者则是实现前者选择的微观手段。文学翻译家在实践中必须根据实际情况，合理地选择归化和异化的立场，灵活地采用直译和意译的译法。在译本创造的实践中，译者很快就会发现：极端的归化或过度的异化都不可取。极端的归化会使源语文化的异国色彩消失殆尽，最终难以达到两种不同文化的交流和融合。而过度的异化则会导致译文晦涩难懂，给文化交流带来困难。归化和异化翻译并不是两种矛盾的、互不相容的策略，各自的具体运用可由作者的意图、文本的类型、翻译的目的和读者的要求这四个因素决定。（郭建中，2003：275）"不论是归化还是异化，也不论是直译还是意译，都可以看作是译者为了适应翻译生态环境所做出的一种翻译策略选择。"（胡庚申，2004：125）总而言之，最重要的是译者需在翻译中把握一个度，既要做到文化间的相互转换与交流，同时又要尽可能地保持各民族文化的多样性与独特性。

## 4. 保留原味的翻译观

德裔美籍民俗学家、翻译家艾伯华（Wolfram Eberhard，1909—1989）出版了三本英文著作，即《中国童话与民间故事》（*Chinese Fairy Tales and Folk Tales*）、《中国民间故事》（*Folktales of China*）与《中国民俗学与相关评论》（*Studies in Chinese Folklore and Related Essays*）。他声明，这几本故事集可能与其他故事书有区别，不那么"审美"，但都是"中国人自己的"，具有中国特点。从前也有不少欧洲人搜集中国故事并将其整理出版成故事集，这些故事都是那些欧洲人在中国土地上听中国人讲的，但由于用欧洲语言转述，因而这些故事多数甚至全部都是用欧洲思维讲述的。这些故事成了一种由欧洲人很不明智地扮演"中国人"来讲中国故事的奇怪的产物，里面掺杂了不少欧洲人自己的见解。尤其是那些被转述的幽默故事，麻烦就更大了。他说，他手里就有这种糟糕的本子，里面有800个故事，能挑出24个像样的就不错了，再一经转译，恐怕剩下的700多个故事也就只有7个能让读者笑出声来。经过翻译或改编的中国故事已经"欧化"，为适应欧洲读者的口味，丧失了中国风格，这种变异是触目惊心的。他强调，他们所收集的中国故事是带有其原有风格和原有价值的，他对3000多个中国故事和多种故事类型进行过短期的田野调查，又经过了科学的工作过程把它们写出来，他的书与此前其他欧洲人的书是不同的。①

北美女传教士费尔德（Adele Marion Fielde，1839—1916）编写中国民间故事集的策略是尽量保持本土化特征。费尔德在《中国夜谭》的再版概述中说道："这本书反映出未受到外国人影响的中国思想，性格是决定一个人或一个民族命运的主要因素，这些故事在它们的起源和目的上完全是本土化的。"这决定了她在搜集民间故事时必须密切贴近民众。只有采用田野作业的调查方式才能够搜集到真正反映本土文化的民间故事，因为任何经过创作的民间文学都不可避免地沾染上作家文学的色彩，而或多或少地失去了本土风味。费尔德采用罗马拼音记录口传的故事，保留了故事文本的本土特点，为后世的西方人来华开展田野调查提供了一个有参考价值的范本。之所以说她是较早地具有民俗学学科意识的西方人，是因为她认识到中国是"民俗学者的理想去处，但迄今为止，人们只探索过它的边界"。她搜集编写的《中国夜谭》可以被看作是首次深入探索中国民间故事的尝试。费尔德倾向于归化和异化相结合的翻译策略，她创作的文本《丢失的箭》体现了这一点。她的译文不仅使中国故事适应本国读者的文化传统，同时还保留了原有故事的文化内核。其中，异化策略体现在文本的译介上，呈现出鲜明的儒家文化特征，具有中国式的社会文化背景，保留了中国人的价值观、婚

---

① 参见董晓萍《翻译与跨文化——解读（德）艾伯华〈中国民间故事类型〉的翻译经过、发现与意义（下）》，载《西北民族研究》2016年第3期，第114–125页。

姻观和民间信仰。归化策略主要体现在人物形象的塑造上。珀尔是费尔德在《丢失的箭》中着力塑造的新女性形象,她敢于突破性别歧视的教育背景,女扮男装进入学堂读书,这是对迂拙守旧的封建文化的反抗;同时,她的婚姻观念也超出了封建制度下包办婚姻的常规,她敢于为自己争取婚姻自由。这些文字折射出西方自由平等的启蒙思想。(胡玥、漆凌云,2020)

## 三、黎族民间文学中经典的选取和翻译

### 1. 原文的选取原则

本书的目的是对黎族民间文学中的经典进行翻译,并对翻译中遇到的问题进行分析和讨论,同时对比英语和汉语在叙事安排以及语言表达方面的差异。黎族民间文学目前有多本汇编,其中符桂花的《黎族民间故事大集》比较有权威性,所选故事较多。该大集的特点是对黎族的民间故事进行了田野采风,然后将其转录成汉字,为每个故事都标注了采风的地点、故事的讲述人以及笔录人,对希望详细了解黎族民间故事的起源和出处的读者来说是一部非常有价值的作品。但是,鉴于本书的重点是翻译和评析,其阅读对象是对民间文学的翻译感兴趣的人群,甚至是国外的英语读者,所以没有必要进行此类标注。

本书中的经典民间故事主要选自《黎族民间故事大集》(海南出版社 2010 年版),另外也有个别故事选自《黎族民间故事选》(上海文艺出版社 1983 年版)。选材的原则是故事要流传广,熟为人知。涵盖的主题包括:人类起源、人神传说、地名由来、名人传奇、节日由来、民俗故事、百姓生活等。此外,在选取故事时,笔者对其中的一些故事进行了再加工和修改,目的是增加叙事的流畅性和文学性,当然,加工的内容并不多。此外,故事原文是在黎语口头叙述的基础上转写而成的,难免存在着明显的口语化特点,在

有些故事的发展过程中，语言有时太过简单，一笔带过，有时转折太快，不符合文学的叙事特点。因此，笔者在整理时对这些明显的地方进行了再加工，目的是理顺上下文的关系，使翻译能够更符合情理。

## 2. 翻译策略的选择

翻译家孙致礼先生提出了"文化传真"的翻译准则。孙先生在20世纪90年代提出，翻译不仅要考虑语言的差异，还要密切注视文化的差异，语言可以转换，甚至可以归化，但文化特色和属性却不宜改变，特别不宜归化，一定要真实地传译出来。（孙致礼，2019：5）所谓"文化传真"，也就是尽量保存外来文化之"洋味"，以使我国读者扩大文化视野，获得知识和启迪。从"文化传真"的目标来看，译文应该是越异化越好；然而，为了照顾读者的接受能力，又不得不容许一定程度的归化。因此，在异化和归化的关系上，孙致礼（1999）认为：文化上要尽量争取异化，尽量避免归化；文字上不得已进行归化时，也要以尽量不引起文化归化为前提。

孙致礼先生的翻译思想是他在几十年翻译实践过程中逐渐沉淀和形成的，正如他自己所总结的，最初的翻译观是发挥译语的优势，倾向于归化的译法，但是后来在修订时都遵循"文化传真"的准则，以异化为主。在他看来，随着中西方文化的交流，当今的读者已经完全适应"洋味"的表达和文化，没有必要进行过度归化而使"文化失真"。他的翻译观给我们带来了很大的启发。

翻译黎族经典民间故事的目的是挖掘其中的民族文化。那么，翻译时遇到典型的问题该怎么处理？处理方法能否形成共性的规律？正是出于这些考虑，我们在翻译时进行了一些思考和总结，并对一些问题进行了探讨和分析，针对每一个故事的特点，聚焦典型问题的探讨。

在翻译过程中，一个突出的问题是术语系统的翻译。例如，对里面的人名和神名的处理，是异化成西方的人名和神名，还是直接用汉语拼音的音译法以保留原来的命名？这两种做法好像都有其道理。异化成西方的人名和神名，其优点在于西方读者易于理解和接受其文化内涵，比如，将山神翻译为 mountain demon。但这也存在问题，如大力神就不能被翻译成 Hercules，因为 Hercules 专指希腊神话中的大力神，与黎族神话系统中的大力神不是一回事。那么，应该将其翻译成 Dali God，还是 God of Strength 呢？如果将其翻译成 God of Strength，就不是专指某一个神，而是一类神，不具有唯一性；但如果将其翻译成 Dali God，那为什么不直接以汉语拼音的形式音译为 Dalishen 呢？其实全部都用汉语拼音的音译法也是有其合理性的，我们可以在初次使用时对其含义加上英文注解，后面再次出现时直接使用汉语拼音。这些神仙是中国黎族神话传说中的神，自成一套神话系统，既不对应于西方神话中的人物，也不对应于中国其他民族神话故事中的人物，因此具有独特的可区别性特征。我们在翻译时，既不能用西方的神话人物去对应他们，又不能凭借意译来阐释他们自身的内涵，因此，最好的办法只能是保持其原有的命名系统，即采用"汉语拼音+注释"的策略。这就像西方的神话人物都有自己的名字，而没有在翻译时被改成其他的名字一样。

  本书所做的工作不是简单的翻译理论的归纳，任何一个既有的翻译理论和方法都无法指导民族文化的翻译，相反，它是个人在翻译过程中对方法和技巧的总结和提炼。在每个故事的翻译过程中，译者都会遇到一些相应的问题，有些涉及句子的顺序调整，有些涉及中西方文化的碰撞，有些涉及深化还是浅化处理，等等。因此，如果拿某一种理论或方法来对应，则是很难成功对号入座的，因为本书涉及的内容和类别比较复杂，不能一概而论。翻译的总体指导思想是在忠实、通顺的总原则的指导下灵活处理，使用包括直译、意译、"汉语拼音+注释"、深化、浅化、弱化、增译、减译、不译等具体的方法和技巧。

# 第四章

## 黎族民间故事译例解析

## 一、专名和通名的区分和翻译

石立坚（1987）对专名和通名进行了较为详细的区分：专名是专用名称的简称，通名是普通名称的简称。专名只是某个单独事物的名称，不是它们所属类别的名称。专名的命名，着眼点在于专名持有者的单独性、个体性、特指性或可鉴别性，不着眼于专名持有者的类别性（种属性）。由专名标记的事物总是独一无二的。与专名对应的是通名，通名既是某个单独事物的名称，同时又是它们所属类别的名称。也可以说，通名是同类事物中不同分子的共用名称。通名命名的着眼点只在于事物的类别性（种属性）。按照这种区分方法，黎族民间故事中那些具有个体属性特指的人物和神都属于专名，他们具有唯一性和不可替代性。而那些个体形象不突出、不具有典型性的名称则可以被归类为通名。在翻译时，对专名应该保留原来的命名，有特定内涵的专名在第一次出现时要采取"汉语拼音+注释"的形式，后面再出现时可以直接使用汉语拼音，以显示这是中国黎族命名系统中的名称；通名的翻译则应突出其意义，因此应该用意译。

### 1. "雷公"的译法

最初，黎族神话中的雷公与其他民族神话中那个脾气暴躁、凶神恶煞的形象不同，他是仁慈和正义的化身，如在《洪水的故事》《黎母山传说》《螃蟹精》《人类的起源》《南瓜的故事》中，雷公是充满正能量的天神，且地位崇高、法力高强，能主宰世间的生死繁衍。韩伯泉（1985）把雷公的作用归纳为三个方面：黎母的降生者、黎民的救世主、撮合兄妹成婚再造黎民的天神。此外，他还把雷公崇拜的原因与海南岛独特的地理位置和气候特征联系在一起，认为海南岛自古以来孤悬海外，古代先民漂洋过海定居于此，受外界文化影响较少，在与大自然斗争的过程中形成了对自然现象的敬

# 第四章
## 黎族民间故事译例解析

畏。海南岛地处热带地区，经常受热带风暴影响，电闪雷鸣是常事，长此以往，黎族人民就形成了对雷公的敬畏，并把他幻化为天神的形象，从而在神话创造中赋予他独一无二的崇高地位。

因此，黎族神话中的雷公是其神话系统中的特指，与其他民族神话中的雷公或雷神并不相同，如果将其翻译为 the Thunder God，就无法区别于其他如汉族民间文学中的雷神。考虑到黎族神话中人名系统的特殊性，最好把它以汉语拼音的形式音译为 Leigong，第一次使用时采取"汉语拼音+注释"的形式译为 Leigong（the Thunder God），后面则直接使用 Leigong。

## 2."黎"的译法

中国有55个少数民族，其英语译名大致分为三类。第一类少数民族英语译名多为汉语拼音，例如：回族 Hui、苗族 Miao、傣族 Dai、傈僳族 Lisu、白族 Bai、景颇族 Jingpo、纳西族 Naxi、怒族 Nu、阿昌族 Achang、畲族 She、德昂族 De'ang、东乡族 Dongxiang、土族 Tu、高山族 Gaoshan、羌族 Qiang、仫佬族 Mulao、毛南族 Maonan、土家族 Tujia、拉祜族 Lahu、仡佬族 Gelao。第二类或因其本身的发音特点，为读音方便或其他缘故而采用了类似于汉语拼音但又有点像英语拼写的译名，例如：满族 Manchu、布朗族 Blang、普米族 Primi、佤族 Va、鄂伦春族 Oroqen、保安族 Bonan、撒拉族 Salar、裕固族 Yugur、塔塔尔族 Tatar、锡伯族 Xibe、独龙族 Derung、基诺族 Jino、布依族 Bouyei、门巴族 Monba、珞巴族 Lhoba、蒙古族 Mongol、达斡尔族 Daur、赫哲族 Hezhen、柯尔克孜族 Kirgiz、鄂温克族 Ewenki。第三类少数民族的聚居地主要位于我国边境，他们有已经固定的英语译名，例如：藏族 Tibetan、朝鲜族 Korean、俄罗斯族 Russian、乌孜别克族 Uzbek。

对上述第一类少数民族，为凸显其少数民族的身份，在英译时除汉语拼音外，往往还加上 people 或 ethnic group，表示×族。因此，黎族一般英译为 the Li people 或者 the Li ethnic group。相应地，本书中黎族的各个分支"杞黎""偀黎""本地黎"是根据地域或方言的不同而形成的不同名称，因此也应该分别以汉语拼音的形式音译。但是，"本地黎"的"本地"为汉语称谓，意思指"土著的黎族"（《中国黎族大辞典》），因此应加注 native Li。

### 3. "黎母"的译法

黎母，虽然从意思来说是黎族人的祖先，应该翻译为 ancestor of the Li people，但是在故事中，这个名字是雷公给她起的，当时她还是一个小姑娘，因此，这个名字是作为一个名称而非一种身份出现的，应该采取汉语拼音音译法，翻译为 Limu。不过，故事的结尾点明黎母是黎族的祖先，因此，除汉语拼音之外，还应采取注释的形式，即 Limu（ancestor of the Li people）。

### 4. "山神"的译法

黎族民间故事中的山神并非一个专名，而是通名，可以指一类神，所以用汉语拼音音译法来翻译并不合适。但若照字面意思翻译为 mountain god，也不符合它的内涵，因为故事里面的山神是吃人的恶魔，应该和雷公等好的神区分开来。因此应改"神"为"魔"，译为 mountain demon，其中 mountain 表示他的生活领地，而 demon 表示他属于恶魔。

### 5. "大力神"的译法

黎族民间故事中的大力神开天辟地，射日月，为民造福，他的作用类似于汉族神话传说中的盘古和后羿，他的地位具有不可替代性，其名称应该属于专名，因此应该按照专名的译法来翻译。虽然英语词汇中的 Hercules 意思也是大力神，也是专名，但其代表的形象却和黎族神话传说中的大力神不一样，他是希腊神话中的一个神，因此绝对不能将黎族民间故事中的大力神翻译为 Hercules，否则会使西方读者产生误解，认为中国的神和希腊的神同属一个体系，这是不恰当的。按照专名翻译的原则，应该将"大力神"翻译为 Dalishen，首次出现时加上注释 God of Strength，意为该神的特点是力气大。

## 二、文化特色词的英译

### 1."俚人"的译法

俚人，是古代生活在百越岭南一带的土著人。自古岭南是俚僚之地，俚僚先民是先秦时的南越部落、西瓯部落及骆越部落人。① 从东汉到魏晋南北朝，广西及越南地区的族群在中原文献中被称为"乌浒""俚""僚"。"俚人"这一称谓出现于隋唐后的文献中。先秦秦汉时期，中原史籍所记载的居住在广西及越南地区的"雒越"，是其最直接的先民。②

故事《冼夫人解救俚女》中的俚女可以翻译成 native girl（土著女孩），崖州俚人则可翻译成 Yazhou people。

### 2."村峒"的译法

"峒"是对古代南方和西南民族群体，也是对广西、贵州、福建部分山区的民族的泛称。早在隋唐以前，南方许多民族往往在山洞中居住，且举峒纯为一姓，保持氏族组织，因此对部分地区的村寨泛称"峒"或"溪峒"，各峒居民被称为"峒蛮"。③ 宋代，黎族社会组织称"峒"，每一宗姓为一峒，全岛黎峒林立但规模较小。明代，黎族地区社会组织仍为村峒，村峒数量较多。清代，在黎族地区建立的土官制主要是在黎族村峒设峒长、总管（或称黎总）、

---

① 《俚人文化》，见搜狗百科网（https://baike.sogou.com/v502581.htm?fromTitle=%E4%BF%9A%E4%BA%BA%E6%96%87%E5%8C%96）。

② 《俚人》，见百度百科网（https://baike.baidu.com/item/%E4%BF%9A%E4%BA%BA%BA）。

③ 《峒》，见百度百科网（https://baike.baidu.com/item/%E5%B3%92/20105099）。

哨官、黎甲、黎长、黎首等职。

故事《冼夫人解救俚女》中冼夫人生活的梁朝比宋代还早几百年，因此，村峒即为自然村寨的意思，翻译为 village。

### 3."黄道婆"的译法

黄道婆（约1245—1330年），又名黄婆、黄母，宋末元初著名的棉纺织家、技术改革家。幼时为童养媳，因不堪虐待流落崖州（今海南省三亚市崖城镇），居约40年，向黎族妇女学习棉纺织技艺并对之进行改进，总结出"错纱、配色、综线、挈花"的织造技术。

黄道婆的原名没有历史记载。在那个动荡的年代，穷苦人家的孩子尤其是女孩子是没有名字的，人们只知道其姓黄，后随夫家姓，黄道婆、黄婆或黄母是她成名后人们对其的尊称。如果把故事中黄道婆的名字都直接译为 Huang Daopo，则不能把这些内涵表达出来。因此，在指称她年轻的时候，应该翻译为 Miss Huang 或 Huang。

例：黄道婆十六岁那年嫁给西厢宋家的第五个儿子宋老五，邻居称她宋五娘。

译文：When Huang was sixteen years old, she married the fifth son of the Song family in the western region and was called Song Wuniang by her neighbors.

## 三、词语的使用与人物形象的塑造问题

在故事《三套神衣》中，三弟是一个机智聪明、敢作敢为、勇往直前的年轻人。为了达到和亚闹结婚的目的，他使用手段偷走了两位哥哥的神衣，但原文并非要批判三弟品质恶劣，而是为了凸显他的机智和勇敢。因此，在翻译时，对原文中几次出现的偷的行为要进行弱化处理。如讲述偷二哥家的猫衣时，译文增加了 he had no way out but to，旨在凸显偷是出于无奈而非其主观意愿；而讲述偷

大哥家的鹰衣时,则直接处理为"He managed to get the 'Eagle costume' from his eldest brother."(他想办法得到了大哥的鹰衣。),偷的意象由此被弱化了。

此外,一些固定用法,如猫的叫声有专门的表达 meow,不能乱用。讲述三弟先后变作老鼠和猫钻进屋里这一情节时,第一次用了 slip into(溜进)来对译"钻",第二次用 duck in(钻进)。因为老鼠身体小,所以很容易就能够溜进去,而猫的身体稍微大一些,从门下面钻进去要低头弓腰,所以用 duck in。至于鼠衣、猫衣、鹰衣的表达,因其有点像戏服,所以用了 costume,而没有用 dress 或者 clothes。此外,山兰酒翻译为 Shanlan rice wine,山兰稻翻译为 Shanlan rice。

## 四、流水句的翻译策略

汉语喜用流水句,而英语喜用显性连接词并注重表达的逻辑性。"流水句"这一名称源于吕叔湘(1979:23—24),他指出"一个小句接一个小句"及"可断可连"是汉语最典型的结构形式。王文斌、赵朝永(2016:17)将流水句的特点扼要概括为句段与句段之间结构松散,不借助显性的关联词语,多个主语或隐或现并常出现跨句段指认,短语和小句共现频繁。流水句具有块状性和离散性,英语句子则具有勾连性和延展性;流水句缺少关联词,而英语句子则需要关联词进行上下句之间的衔接和连贯。英汉两种语言的结构形式存在本质差异,翻译时应注意进行调整,尤其是要对流水句进行适当拆分,找到句子的主语和每句话之间的逻辑关系,并加上适当的衔接词。

例1:伏波将军射断尖峰之后,马不停蹄,翻山越岭,勇往直前。

该句子的主语看似是伏波将军,即伏波将军射断尖峰,伏波将军马不停蹄,伏波将军翻山越岭,伏波将军勇往直前,但实际上句子讲的却是伏波将军率领军队的事情。汉语表达含蓄、笼统，但翻译成英语时，必须加上对应的主语，因为英语是形合性的语言，语言表达要有逻辑性，一个句子必须有明确的主语和谓语动词，否则就不是一个完整的句子。因此，在翻译时，要添加逻辑主语。原句子完整的表达应该是：伏波将军射断尖峰之后，伏波将军率领军队马不停蹄，翻山越岭，勇往直前。因为射断尖峰的情节在前面已经翻译过，此处简略表达为"此后"（after that），将"马不停蹄"翻译成 without a single halt（片刻不休息）。整句译文为："After that, he commanded the army to climb the mountains without a single halt."。

例2：飞马来到感恩县的沙滩地带时，日正当午，烈日笼笼，人马都渴得不可开交。

该句的逻辑主语不只是飞马，而是包含了整个军队，因此，翻译时省略飞马，而译为"当他们来到……"（when they came to…）。"日正当午"也是汉语的表述习惯，在英语中，时间状语应该放在句子末尾，因此，应调整整个句子的顺序以符合英语的表达习惯，组合成一个时间状语从句"当他们在中午到达……时，烈日笼笼，人马渴得要死"。完整的译文为："When they came to the beach of Gan'en County at noon, the sun was so hot that both soldiers and horses were thirsty to death."。

例3：他们痛饮清泉，清甜透肺，精神倍增，胜利班师回朝。

该句蕴含了好几层意思，拆分开来是：他们痛饮清甜透肺的清泉之后精神倍增，从而赢得胜利，胜利后班师回朝。因此，翻译时宜按照英语的表述习惯把句子的语序重组并译为："Aftering drinking the sweet and clear spring water, both soldiers and horses were energetic again. As a result, they achieved victory effortlessly."。

## 五、情歌的翻译

黎族民间故事里穿插了很多男女对唱的情歌，这些情歌通常是青年男女对对方爱慕之情的表达，这或许是因为情话难以直接说出，而通过歌唱更能尽情表达。由于这些情歌是黎族人唱出来的原汁原味的歌曲，其中有很多原生态表达，包括方言词汇和句子结构等，翻译时都应该进行斟酌。

## 1. 对称谓进行变译

在黎族情歌中，青年男女通常用"阿哥""阿妹"来称呼对方，男对女的称谓是阿妹，女对男的称谓是阿哥，两者蕴含的是"亲爱的"的意思。英译时应该按照西方人的习惯，将称谓处理为 my love 或者 my dear，而不能简单地对应英语中的 sister 和 brother，因为 sister 在英语中表示"姐妹；护士长；修女；女教友；亲密女友"，brother 表示"兄弟；基督会教友；同人；同事；黑人兄弟"，除完全没有与汉语同等的含义外，还会引起误解。

## 2. 对喻体进行变译

黎族情歌还喜欢使用比喻，喻体通常为他们熟悉的事物，如故事《鹿回头村》里的情歌"妹歌似天调，靓过鹦哥鸟，今日捡得宝，木棉开花苞"，其中用了"天调""鹦鹉""木棉花"来进行比喻。"天调"是形容女子的歌声好听，因此可以直接翻译成"Your song is so sweet."，而非"Your song is like the tune from the heaven."；"鹦鹉"（parrot）在英语中的联想义是"学舌的人"，并非正面的意象，因此翻译时不能把女子美丽的歌声和鹦鹉比，而应该将其归化为英语中的 nightingale（夜莺），因为夜莺在英语中的意象是能唱优美的歌曲的鸟儿，英国诗人济慈的《夜莺颂》、小说家王尔德的《夜莺与玫瑰》都反映了这一意象的内涵。

## 3. 尽量做到押韵

黎族民歌还讲究韵律，如故事《鹿回头村》里面的情歌对唱："阿哥好仪表，侬想把心交，阿哥有胆量，做吃肯耐劳。// 妹从哪里来？肉菜①如此好？此样好容貌，做乜来相找？// 五指山神女，小名叫阿娇，阿哥要吃水，妹愿做水瓢。// 妹歌似天调，靓过鹦哥鸟，今日捡得宝，木棉开花苞。// 阿哥人枯燥，孤单静悄悄，夜给哥铺席，日替哥守寮。"整体上押的是"ao"韵，读起来朗朗上口，翻译时也应当尽量押韵，体现出黎族歌谣的音韵美。该段情歌对话英译如下：

My dear is strong and handsome,
I'd like to give my heart to him.
My dear is courageous,
And hardworking all the time.
  Where are you from?
  Like a flower in blossom,
  Such a beautiful lady,
  Where can I find?
Goddess of Wuzhishan Mountain,
My nickname is Ajiao.
If my dear wants water,
I would like to be a ladle.
  Your song is so sweet,
  Even sweeter than a nightingale,
  Today I got a treasure,
  And Kapok blossoms in full.
My dear will not be alone;
My dear won't be lonely any more.
I will make bed for you at night,
And wait at home in the daytime.

---

① 指身体丰满健康。

# 第五章

## 黎族经典民间故事汉英对照

## 故事一　人类的起源

很久很久以前，地上长着一个葫芦瓜。它不断长大，长得比山还要高大。雷公把葫芦瓜开了个口，把用泥土捏成的哥妹两人放进去，又把泥土捏成的水牛、黄牛、猪、狗、猫、四脚蛇、螳螂等动物一雌一雄地放进去。当时暴发了一次大洪水，葫芦瓜随着洪水漂流。洪水退去后，天上出了五个太阳、五个月亮，很快就把水晒干了。经过太阳、月亮和水的作用，葫芦瓜内的泥人和其他泥动物都变活了，跳了出来，只觉得天气热，太阳晒在身上像火烤一样。晚上，当月亮出来后，月光亮得人连眼睛也睁不开的时候，神仙就问道："谁能把太阳和月亮去掉几个呢？"山猪应着说："我的牙齿长，可以去吃掉它们。"哥哥和妹妹叫山猪快点去吃，可是山猪说："想要我吃掉它们，你们要给我稻吃才行。"哥哥和妹妹都答应了，并说："五个太阳晒得太热了，你吃掉四个吧。"山猪便去把四个太阳吃掉了，把四个月亮咬碎了，月亮变成许多星星。山猪回来了，可是当时没有稻给它吃，兄妹两人只得许诺它说："这样吧，你以后看见哪里有稻就到哪里吃好了。"所以，现在山猪到处吃人们种的稻子。

那时候，哥哥和妹妹看见到处都是荒芜的土地，他们走过了一座又一座山，走过了一条又一条河，到处都找不到一个人，不禁哭了起来。恰好天上的雷公从这里经过，听见了哭声，就下来问他们为什么哭。他们说："现在世上只有我们兄妹俩。到处都是荒山野岭，到处都是荒草杂树，今后怎样过日子呢？"雷公说："不要怕，我帮助你们。这样好了，你们就结成夫妻吧！"兄妹俩听他这样说，急了起来，忙说："不行，我们是兄妹，不能成为夫妻，雷公会劈死我们的。"雷公说："你们不要怕，我就是雷公，不会劈你们。"

他们只是摇头,并不相信。雷公为了使他们相信,就发起威来。一会儿,天上响起"隆隆"的声音,一阵比一阵更响,震得地也动起来。不久,只见河水被分开,树木被劈倒。雷公笑着对他们说:"看见了吧?相信我好了。"于是,他们听雷公的话,结成了夫妻。后来妹妹生了一个男孩,长得白白胖胖的,夫妻俩欢喜无限。这时雷公来了,问他们:"你们日子过得很好吧?生小孩了吗?交给我吧。"他们心里慌了起来,忙说道:"还没有生孩子。"雷公说:"已经生了,我知道了,交给我吧,我可以变出很多人来,你们就不会愁没有人了。"他们不肯将孩子交出来,雷公只得抢抱出来,他们急得抱头大哭。雷公把小孩砍碎,然后用筛子来筛,只见筛出的肉块一下子就变成四个男子和四个女子。雷公把衣服给他们穿,第一个男子穿上衫和裤,便成为汉族人。要给第二个男子时,布不够了,只能给两块布片,前后各一块系在腰间遮盖下体,做成"吊裆裤"穿,这个便成为"杞黎"。等到给第三个男子时,布更少了,只能做成三角裤的样子,这个便成为"侾黎"。最后一个男子只得一小块布,做成的三角裤比"侾黎"的还要小,这个便成为"本地黎"。四个男子和四个女子相配成婚,以后生子生孙,子子孙孙一代一代地生存下来。

## The Origin of Human Being

A long time ago, there was a gourd melon on the ground. It kept growing till it was taller than a mountain. Leigong (the Thunder God) cut the gourd and put the clay-made brother and sister into it, as well as the male and female clay-made buffalos, oxen, pigs, dogs, cats, four-legged snakes, mantises and so on. When the flood water came, the gourd melon drifted in the water. After the flood water receded, five suns and five moons appeared in the sky, and the water was quickly dried. Affected by the suns, the moons and the water, the clay-made brother and sister as well as other animals in the gourd melon became alive. They jumped out of the gourd melon just feeling that the weather was too hot, with the sun bathing on the body just like being scorched by fire. In the evening, when the moons came out, the moonlight was so bright that they even could not open their eyes. The immortal asked, "Who can remove the suns and the moons?" A wild boar replied, "My teeth are long, and I can go and eat them." The brother and the sister asked the wild boar to do it as soon as possible, but the wild boar asked them to promise that they would provide it with rice as food after it did that job. Both the brother and the sister agreed, and asked the wild boar to eat four of the five suns as it was too hot. Then the wild boar ate four suns, and crushed four moons into many twinkling stars. But when the wild boar came back, there was no rice for it to eat. The brother and the sister had to make a promise that the wild boar could go anywhere it could find rice and eat it from then on. Therefore, nowadays, wild boars eat rice grown by people everywhere.

At that time, uncultivated land was everywhere. The brother and the sister climbed over one mountain after another and waded through one river after another but could find no other people. They felt depressed and could not help crying. It happened that Leigong was passing by and heard the cry. He came down and asked why they cried. The brother and the sister said, "There are only the two of us in the world, with wild mountains and grasses everywhere. How can we live in the future?" Leigong replied, "Don't worry. I will help you. Well, you can marry each other!" Hearing these words, the brother and the sister were astonished and said, "We cannot marry each other because we are brother and sister. If so, Leigong will strike us with lightning." Leigong consoled them and said, "Do not be afraid. I am Leigong. I will not punish you." They just shook their heads and didn't believe it. In order to convince them, Leigong began to show his strong power. For a moment, rumbling sound came from the sky, and it became louder and louder with the ground shaking badly. Soon a river was separated and trees were struck. Then Leigong said smilingly, "See? Now believe me." So they followed Leigong's words and got married. Later, the sister gave birth to a chubby baby boy, and the couple were very happy. Just then, Leigong came and asked, "Do you enjoy a happy life and have a baby? Now give him to me." They became panicky and said, "We have no baby yet." Leigong replied, "I know you have given birth to a baby boy. Give him to me, and I can conjure a lot of people out of him, then you will not be lonely." They refused to hand over the baby, so Leigong had to grab the baby from them. They cried anxiously. Leigong chopped the baby into pieces and sieved them. Suddenly the sifted meat pieces turned to be four men and four women. Leigong dressed them. The first man was given clothes and a pair of trousers to wear and he became a Han people. When it came to the second man, the cloth was not enough, so he was given two pieces of cloth, one piece to cover the waist and another to cover the lower part of the body. The second man was the ancester of "Qi Li". The third man was provided with even less cloth, which could only be made into briefs. The third man was the ancester of "Xiao Li". The last man was given only a small piece of cloth to make the briefs which was even smaller. That man became the ancester of "Bendi Li" (native Li). The four men and the four women got married and had children. Their offspring became different branches of the ethnic groups on Hainan Island.

**故事二 黎母的神话**

相传海南岛的黎族人是黎母所生的。

在远古年代，在海南岛思河的上游有一座高山，经常云雾缠绕，看不见它的真面目。那时，这里还没有人。有一天，雷公经过这里。雷公是天上的天神，主宰天地的一切，发现这一带既有山，又有水，是繁殖人种的好地方，便把一颗蛇卵放在这座山中。海南天气炎热，经过九千九百九十九个日夜，蛇卵发出一声响，卵壳里跳出一个女孩子来。这个女孩长得活泼可爱，她住在山洞中，天鸟天天叼树果来喂养她。她长到十八岁，就自己采野果果腹，夜晚睡在树上。雷公给她起了个名字，叫黎母。黎母就在山里生活下来。

后来，有一个由外地渡海来到这座大山里采沉香的青年，被山神擒拿，囚在铁笼里，山神准备杀死他腌肉吃。黎母发现后，给他送水解渴，这青年央求黎母姑娘搭救他。黎母心地善良，去和雷公商量，雷公拔下牙齿赠给黎母，嘱咐她如此如此。不久，雷公又是霹雷，又是闪电，把囚着那青年的铁笼劈开。黎母把那青年拉到由雷公的牙齿变成的小船上。这时只见洪水漫天盖地而来，山神等恶魔被冲下大海，只有小船漂在水上。洪水退后，黎母和那采沉香的青年安然无恙。这时雷公一声吼："你们俩就成亲吧！"于是，他们俩便结婚，在山上一起生活，向雷公借来火种，刀耕火种，种植了山兰稻。他们后来生了许多子女，子女又生孙子女，这些子孙就是后来的黎族百姓。黎母和那采沉香的青年死后，就被葬在那座山上，子孙后代为了纪念自己的祖先，便把这座山叫作黎母山。

# The Legend of Limu[①]

According to legend, the Li people of Hainan Island were offspring of Limu.

In ancient times, there was a mountain in the upper reaches of the Sihe River on Hainan Island. Often entangled in clouds, the mountain could hardly be seen. There were no human beings on the island. One day, Leigong, the Thunder God who dominated everything in the heaven and the earth, passed by and found this area which was covered with mountain and water a suitable place for breeding people, so he put a snake egg in the mountain. Due to the hot weather of Hainan Island all year round, after 9999 days and nights' incubation, the snake egg burst apart with a bang and a girl came out of the egg shell. The girl was very lovely. She lived in a cave and was fed by the birds with fruit from trees every day. When she was 18 years old, she began to feed herself by picking wild fruit and sleep on tree branches at night. Leigong named her Limu and Limu continued to live in the mountains.

One day, a young man, who crossed the sea and came to the mountain area to pick up eaglewood, was caught by the mountain demon. The demon imprisoned the young man in a cage and was about to kill him and pickle him as food. Limu found him and brought him water to quench his thirst. When the young man begged Limu to rescue him, she was touched and went to Leigong for help. Leigong pulled out one of his teeth and told Limu what to do. After a while, Leigong used thunder and lightning bolt to strike the cage and the young man was liberated. Then Limu and the young man got onto the boat which was conjured from

---

① Ancestor of the Li people.

Leigong's tooth. Suddenly, heavy flooding came and all the demons such as the mountain demon were drowned, only leaving the boat floating on the water. After the flood water receded, Limu and the young man were safe and sound. Leigong asked them to get married and live together, they did so and lived on the mountain. They used stone to till the land and cultivated mountain rice which was later known as Shanlan rice. They also borrowed fire from Leigong and learned to keep and use it. Later, they had many descendants, who were known as the Li people. After Limu and her husband died, they were buried on the mountain. In order to commemorate them, their descendants called the mountain the Limu Mountain.

## 故事三　万家——关于山区和平原的传说

自从大地发生了滔天洪水，土地都是湿漉漉的，人们生活很困难。有一个人，名字叫万家，他为了使土地干爽起来，让人们可以在土地上自由来往，便造了五个太阳、五个月亮，挂在天上。五个太阳、五个月亮都是热烘烘的，七棱八角，不方不圆。它们发出毒热的光芒，不到两三天，土地都被晒得干裂了，树木都被晒得枯焦了；人们在屋子里热得坐卧不宁，一出门便被晒得半死。因此，人们就来要求万家除掉四个太阳和四个月亮。

万家看见太阳和月亮对人民不利，就答应了大家的要求，拿起弓箭，跑到屋子后面的高山顶上，鼓足气力，向太阳和月亮射去。他一连射了八支箭，四个太阳和四个月亮便从空中落下来了。从此天空中便只有一个太阳和一个月亮。

由于洪水冲、太阳晒，地上积成了许多山岭、石块。武艺高超、心地善良的万家又造了一张很大的耙，造了一头很大很大的牛，给人们耙地，把石块和大山都耙到大海里去。他先在文昌、琼山①一带耙，造出了许多平原；然后在东方、白沙等地耙。正在耙的时候，耙齿坏了几根，耙得不干净了，许多石头、高山都从坏了的耙齿里漏出来。因此，东方、白沙、琼中、保亭一带成了一片山多石多的山区地带。

---

① 文昌在海南岛的东部，琼山在东北部，东方、白沙在西部，琼中、保亭在中部。

## Wanjia: A Legend About Mountains and Plains

After the great flood engulfed the earth, the land became so wet that people lived a hard life. A man named Wanjia wanted to dry the land and enable people to move freely on the ground, so he created five suns and five moons and hung them in the sky. With irregular shapes, the suns and the moons radiated a huge amount of heat, so within a couple of days, the land was dried up and the trees were scorched. Besides, people were restless in their house and would be roasted to death if they went outside. Therefore, people asked Wanjia to get rid of four suns and four moons.

Realizing that the suns and the moons had got people in trouble, Wanjia agreed to their request. He picked up his bows and arrows, ran to the top of the mountain behind his house, and summoned up the energy to shoot at the suns and the moons. After Wanjia shot eight arrows in a row, four suns and four moons fell from the sky. From then on, there was only one sun and one moon in the sky.

Due to the flood and the sun, many mountains and hills were accumulated on the ground. The powerful and kind-hearted Wanjia made a huge harrow and created a giant cow to rake the mountains and hills into the sea. Initially, he raked in Wenchang and Qiongshan[①] and created many plains. Then when Wanjia began to rake in Dongfang, Baisha and other places, some of the rake teeth were broken so some mountains and hills were left there without being raked. Therefore, Dongfang, Baisha, Qiongzhong and Baoting became mountainous regions.

---

① Wenchang is in the east of Hainan Island; Qiongshan is in the northeast; Dongfang and Baisha are in the west; Qiongzhong and Baoting are in the middle.

## 故事四 伟代①造动物

据说在远古时候，大地上的情况和现在不同。那时人是不会死的，老了又可慢慢变年轻，地面上的石头也和活的东西一样，会不断长大，因此，石头越来越多，把人们耕种的田地都占据了。眼看生活不能维持下去，于是，天上的伟代发下一次大水，把整个地面都淹没了。

在洪水发生之前，伟代预先把今天我们所见的各种动物，如人、山猪、蚂蚁、狗、牛、鸡等进行雌雄配对，放进一个大瓜壳里，让它在洪水到来时随水漂流。洪水过后，地面上所有的动物都淹死了，只剩下瓜壳内的各对雌雄动物，从此延续后代，成为今天的动物世界。

当洪水初退的时候，地面很是湿软，所有动物都站不住脚，于是，伟代便造了五个太阳把地面晒干。躲在瓜壳里的动物开始往外面跑，最先跑出来的是黄猄。黄猄被五个太阳晒得透不过气来，热得四处乱跑，结果额头碰到石壁上，裂开了一道痕。因此，今天我们看见的黄猄额上都有一道白痕。接着，黄牛出来了。黄牛被太阳晒得难受，只得跑上山去躲避，但皮已经被太阳晒红了。因此，今天的黄牛全身都是红色的，而且被放牧在山上。跟着跑出来的是水牛。水牛更怕热，就躲到水潭里。潭里的污泥把它的身体都染成了黑色。因此，今天的水牛都是黑皮肤的，而且喜欢浸在水里。然后，山猪跑出来了。山猪也怕热，便钻入泥穴里，把身体弄得脏脏的。因此，今天的山猪全身都长着黑茸茸的毛。最后走出来的是山马。它先露出半截身体，不经意地东张西望，不料身体很快便被太

---

① 黎族传说中的创造万物的全能者。

阳晒红了,它赶紧跑进深山里去躲避。因此,今天的山马后半截身体还是黑色的。

# Weidai[①] Creating Animals

According to legend, in ancient times, the condition on the earth was totally different from that of today. People used to be immortal. After getting old, they would rejuvenate again. Besides, stones on the ground could also grow up like living things. Therefore, more and more stones occupied human being's farmland. Seeing that it was difficult for people to maintain their lives, Weidai from heaven created a great flood to overwhelm the earth.

Before the flood, Weidai paired various animals including human beings, such as boars, ants, dogs, cattle, chickens and so on, and put them into a large melon shell. When the flood came, the melon shell were carried along by the water. All animals on the ground were drowned in the flood except for those which were hidden in the melon shell. From then on, those paired animals began to reproduce, and thus formed the current animal world.

When the flood water began to recede, the muddy ground was too soft and slippery to stand on, so Weidai created five suns to dry the ground. With the suns baking the melon shell, the animals that were hiding in it couldn't bear and started to run out of the shell. The first animal running out of the shell was a muntjac that ran about restlessly and hit its forehead severely on the stone wall. As a result, a scar was left on its forehead. Therefore, all muntjacs we see today have a white

---

[①] Weidai was an almighty god who was able to create everything in the legend of the Li nationality.

scar on their foreheads. The second animal running out of the melon shell was an ox, which felt uncomfortably hot outside and hid in a mountain. As it had got sunburned, its skin became maroon. That's why the oxen today are maroon all over their bodies and grazed on mountains. Following the ox was a buffalo. The buffalo was even more afraid of the hotness, so it hid in a water pool. As a result, its body was dyed dark by the mud in the pool. That's why buffaloes' skin are dark and they enjoy soaking in the pool today. Then the boar ran out of the melon shell. The boar was also afraid of the heat outside, so it burrowed into the mud hole, making its body dirty. As a result, boars today have black fur all over their bodies. The last animal coming out of the melon shell was a sambar which showed its upper body to look around and got its upper body burned red by the strong sunlight. Then the sambar ran into a mountain hurriedly. Consequently, the lower bodies of sambars remain black today.

## 故事五　大力神

远古时候，天地相距只有几丈远。天上有七个太阳和七个月亮，把大地烧得滚烫，像个大热锅。白天，生灵都躲到深洞里去避暑；夜间，人们也不敢出来。只有在日月交替的黎明和黄昏，人们才争先恐后地走出洞口去找一些吃的。大家都叫苦连天。

有一个大力神，他想：这样挨日子，叫人们怎样活下去？于是，他在一夜之间使出了他的全部本领：把身躯伸高一万丈，把天空拱高一万丈。

天空被拱高了，但天上还有七个太阳和七个月亮，热烘烘的。于是，大力神做了一把很大的硬弓和许多支利箭。白天，他冒着猛烈的阳光去射太阳，一箭一个地把六个太阳射落了下来。当他准备射第七个太阳的时候，人们纷纷说："留下这最后一个吧！世间万物生长离不开太阳呢！"大力神答应了人们的请求，留下了一个太阳。夜晚，大力神又冒着刺眼的强光去射月亮。他张弓搭箭，射落了六个月亮，射第七个月亮的时候，因为射偏了，只射缺了一小片。当他准备重射时，人们又纷纷说："饶了它吧！让它把黑暗的夜间照亮。"大力神又答应了人们的请求。这样，月亮后来便有时候圆，有时候缺。

大力神拱天射日月以后，心想：平展展的一片大地，光溜溜的，没有山川和森林，人们又怎样生息繁衍呢？于是，他从天上取下彩虹当作扁担，拿来地上的道路当作绳索，从海边挑来沙土造山垒岭。从此，大地上便出现了高山峻岭，那大大小小的山丘，是从他的大筐里漏下来的泥沙。他还把梳下来的头发往群山上撒，山上便长出如头发般茂密的森林，山上的鸟兽们都非常感激大力神为它们造林筑巢的恩德。

有了山岭，还得造鱼虾等生息的江河湖泊。大力神拼尽力气，用脚尖踢划群山，凿通了无数的沟谷，他的汗水流淌在这些谷里，便形成了奔腾的江河。这中间最大的一条，就是从五指山一直流入南海的昌化江！

大力神为万物生息不辞劳苦，完成造化万物后，已经筋疲力尽，他终于倒了下来。临死前，他还生怕天再倒塌下来，所以撑开巨掌，高高举起，把天牢牢地顶住。传说，那巍然屹立的五指山，就是黎族祖先的英雄——大力神的巨手！

# Dalishen[①]

In ancient times, the heaven and the earth were only several feet away from each other, and there were seven suns and seven moons in the sky, burning the earth and making it like a big hot pot. During the day time, all creatures hid in deep caves to get rid of the hotness. Even at night, they did not dare to come out. Only at dawn and dusk when day and night alternated, people could rush out of the cave and try to find something to eat. Everyone complained.

Dalishen wanted to help people escape such a bad situation. He tried his best overnight to stretch his body to 10000 feet high so that the sky was pushed 10000 feet higher away from the ground.

Although the sky was lifted far away from the ground from then on, those seven suns and seven moons were still bathing the earth. Then, Dalishen made a great hard bow and many arrows. During the day time, he shot at the suns one by one in the dazzling sunshine. After six suns had been shot down, people begged him, "Leave one sun please, for everything in the world can't grow without the sun." Thus Dalishen

---

① God of Strength.

agreed with their request and left one sun in the sky. At night, he shot at the moons one by one in the glaring moonlight, and six moons were shot down with six arrows perfectly. When shooting the seventh moon, the arrow was off-tracked and only a small piece of the moon was split out. When he was preparing for a re-shoot, people pleaded, "Please leave it there to light up the dark night." The god agreed to people's request and left the moon there. That's why the moon has its waxing and waning days.

Having raised the sky and shot down six suns and six moons, the god began to make people a better living place by turning such flat and bare land into mountains or forests. Taking rainbow from the sky as shoulder pole and roads on the ground as ropes, he carried silt from seaside to build mountains. Since then, there were mountains. The silt leaked from his huge baskets turned into hills and mounds. He also sprinkled his hair on the mountains and turned it into lush forests. The birds and beasts on the mountains all thanked Dalishen for making such a good living place for them.

Then he began to make rivers and lakes to breed aquatic creatures. Dalishen kicked the mountains very hard and cut out many valleys with his tiptoes. His sweat flowing down through the valleys became rushing rivers. The largest river among them was the Changhuajiang River flowing from the Wuzhishan Mountain to the South China Sea.

The god spared no effort and toiled for all creatures. When things were all done, he was exhausted to death. For fear that the sky would fall down again, he lifted his giant palms and held the sky firmly before he breathed his last breath. Legend has it that the great Wuzhishan Mountain is the giant hand of Dalishen, the hero of the Li ancestors.

## 故事六 雷公根

在美丽富饶的七指岭脚下，有个村寨，寨里有个名叫打占的青年，他身体魁梧，为人正直。因此，他不但在世上有很多的朋友，天上的雷公也和他结交朋友，雷公还教会了他上天的本领。

有一次，雷公邀请打占上天做客。在酒席上，雷公问打占："天下的人最怕什么？"不等打占回答，雷公就站起身来摇动大鼓，一时鼓声隆隆，雷公好不得意。雷公摇罢，又问打占："这声音天下的黎民百姓都怕吗？"打占回答说："只是震耳罢了。"

不久，打占回请雷公，雷公很高兴来到人间。打占在火塘边热情地接待雷公，按照黎家的风俗习惯，敬了雷公九大碗糯米酒，为雷公洗尘。酒后，打占站了起来，从火塘边的火架顶上拿下了红白藤条和豹尾，在地上"啪啪"地猛抽猛打，藤条和豹尾与地面相碰，迸出一阵阵耀眼的火星。雷公眼见这一宝贝厉害得很，心中害怕，但不愿自灭威风，便摇摇脑袋表示不怕。

次日早晨，打占牵着牛犁田去了。雷公起床之后，看见架顶上放着的豹尾和藤条，起了贪心。他心里想：如果把这些宝贝弄回去，轰轰的响声和刺眼的强光我就都有了，天底下的人就一定会更怕我！于是，他慌忙从架顶上拿了藤条和豹尾，驾着云头飞上九天。打占回到家里，发现雷公偷走了他的豹尾和藤条，举起钩刀"嗖"的一声，飞步冲上天去追赶雷公。雷公看见打占追来，心里十分慌张，赶忙施展本领，赶快逃跑，一直跑到南天门，想钻进天府里去。打占也是紧紧追赶，毫不放松，就在雷公要跨进门槛时，一把抓住雷公的左脚。雷公嚎叫着："放开我！放开我！"打占哪里肯放，他紧紧抓住雷公，气呼呼地说："要放你，先得把东西还我！还我！"两人正相持不下的时候，南天门的管门神来了，他看见雷公把凡人带上天来，赶紧关起天门。雷公被夹在门缝里呱呱直叫，死劲地往门内钻。打占手脚快，他拔出钩刀，用力一砍，一下子就把夹在门外的雷公的左脚砍了下来。

打占拿着雷公的左脚，在天门外游荡了七七四十九天，寻找雷公算账。但天门紧闭，他无法进去，只好把雷公的左脚拿回家里用刀一节节剁下来。他每剁一下，雷公在天上就忍着一阵剧痛，擂打一阵大鼓，抽打一阵藤条和豹尾。于是，天上便发出阵阵的电闪和雷鸣。

打占把雷公的左脚剁烂了，又架起土锅，将脚肉放在锅里烧，烧熟后把它吃掉，让雷公永世残废。正当打占大口大口地吃着雷公的脚肉时，突然感到一股苦味。打占一气之下，连锅带肉全都倒在田埂上。经七七四十九天，田埂上忽然长出了一种叶子圆圆的植物。后来，人们就叫它为雷公根。

## **Leigonggen**

  Long long ago, there was a village at the foot of the beautiful and prosperous Qizhiling Mountain. In the village there was a young man named Dazhan. Dazhan was tall, strong and upright. Therefore, not only did he have many friends in the human world, but also he made friends with Leigong, the Thunder God of the heaven, who even taught him how to get to the heaven.

  One day, Leigong invited Dazhan to visit him in the heaven. At the banquet, Leigong asked Dazhan what people in the human world fear the most. Without waiting for an answer, Leigong stood up and beat the drum. For a moment, the drum rumbled and Leigong was very satisfied. Then Leigong asked Dazhan if people in the human world feared that sound. "It's just earsplitting," answered Dazhan.

  Shortly afterwards, Dazhan gave a return banquet to Leigong.

Leigong was very happy to come to the human world. In accordance with the customs of the Li people, Dazhan warmly welcomed Leigong by the Chinese fireplace. He toasted Leigong nine bowls of glutinous rice wine to show his respect. After drinking the wine, Dazhan stood up, took the red and white rattan whip and the leopard tail from the top of the hob beside the Chinese fireplace, and beat them fiercely on the ground. The rattan whip and leopard tail collided with the ground, bursting out bright sparks. Leigong was afraid of this grisliness thing in heart, but was unwilling to admit it, so he shook his head to show that he was not afraid of it.

Early next morning, Dazhan led the cattle to plough the fields. When Leigong got up, he saw the leopard tail and rattan whip on top of the shelf and became greedy. He thought that if he got such precious things, he would have both the roar sound and the dazzling light, and people in the human world would definitely be more afraid of him. So he hurriedly grasped the rattan whip and leopard tail from the top of the shelf and flew up to the heaven. When Dazhan returned home, he found that Leigong had stolen his leopard tail and rattan whip, so he raised his hook knife and flew in a rush to the sky to catch up with Leigong. Leigong saw Dazhan coming and felt very nervous. He rushed to flee to the south gate of the heaven, trying to get into the heavenly palace, but Dazhan followed him closely. When Leigong was about to step into the threshold, Dazhan caught Leigong's left foot. Leigong shouted, "Let me go! Let me go!" How would Dazhan let him go? He grasped the foot more tightly and said angrily, "If you want me to let you go, you must return my things first! Give them back to me!" When they were in struggle, the god in charge of guarding the south gate came. Seeing Leigong bring the mortal to the heaven, he quickly shut the door of the heavenly palace. Leigong was clamped in the crack of the door and squeaked, squeezing hard into the heavenly palace, with his left foot clipped by the door. Dazhan pulled out his hook knife and cut off Leigong's left foot.

Taking Leigong's left foot, Dazhan wandered outside the gate of the heavenly palace for forty-nine days, trying to find Leigong. But the gate was closed and he could not enter, so he had to take Leigong's left foot home and cut it into pieces with knife. Every time he chopped the foot, Leigong felt a sharp pain in the sky, and he would beat the drum as well as the rattan whip and leopard tail. Thus there were bursts of lightning and thunder in the sky.

Dazhan chopped up Leigong's left foot and cooked the foot meat in an earthen pot so as to make Leigong cripple forever. When Dazhan tried to eat Leigong's foot meat, he felt a bitter taste. Dazhan was very angry and dumped the pot and meat on the field ridge. Forty-nine days later, a round-leafed plant sprouted from the field ridge. Later, people began to call it Leigonggen.

## 故事七　兄弟星座

传说很早以前，在一座无名大山里居住着一户有着七兄弟的人家。他们的父母虽然早已去世，但他们和睦相处，团结友爱，日子过得很安稳。

他们以种山兰稻为生。有一年，七兄弟为了种山兰，砍了整整一天山。当他们砍到山腰上那棵天芋树①时，天已经暗了下来，他们只好收拾砍刀回家去。

第二天一早，他们来到山上，见到那些已经被砍倒的树木和粗藤又长起来了，觉得很奇怪。他们又辛辛苦苦地砍了一整天。第三天，他们上山一看，那些被砍倒的树藤又全都长了起来。他们感到更加奇怪了。天黑之后，他们分散在树林里躲了起来。半夜时分，只见天上闪出一片白光，接着从那棵天芋树上跳下来一只大天猪，在他们已经砍光的树木杂草地甩喷出一缕白烟，口中念念有词："塞呀塞，云呀云，合东灵东灵。"② 这时候，那些被砍倒的树木和粗藤又重新长好，复活了过来。那天猪便跳上天芋树，回到天上去了。

七兄弟决定用大木头做一把几个人才能拉得动的大弓和一支很大很大的箭，装在天芋树下面，并发誓：杀死天猪之后，要上天去找玉帝算账。

这一天，兄弟七人又齐心协力砍了一天，天黑了，他们躲在天芋树底下。待到下半夜，又见那天猪呼哧呼哧地走下来，刚喷出白烟，七兄弟便拉开弓，搭上箭，嗖的一声，一箭射中天猪的肚皮。

---

① 天芋树：相传古代有一棵高入云天的天芋树，是天地之间的桥架。后来被七弟用肉汤泼在花蕊上骤然缩成现在常见的山芋。

② 塞呀塞，云呀云，合东灵东灵：黎语，意思是树呀树，藤呀藤，各归其原吧。

它慌忙跳上芋秆，直往天上奔去。那七兄弟毫不放松，扛起木犁顺着血迹追上天庭。

到了天上，只见一排排仙宫琼阁矗立在云雾之中。他们一直追到玉帝的猪栏里，见一只小山般的大猪已死在那里，便吵到天宫，要同玉帝算账。玉帝被他们吵醒了，来见他们，问道："喂，小伙子们，你们吵什么呀？"

七兄弟理直气壮地说："万界①，你的猪窜到人间，把我们几天里砍的山兰坡地都糟蹋了，我们找你算账！"

玉帝回答说："啊，好哇，既然它犯了天规，私下凡间而被你们猎中，万界我现在把它交给你们处置。不过必须把它全部吃完，不能剩下一星半点。"

于是，他们燃起冲天烈火，七把尖刀对着天猪一齐开剐，没有多少工夫，便把猪肉吃了个精光，只剩下一瓢肉汤。这时，七弟随手把它往芋蕊上一泼。刹那工夫，只见那顶天立地的芋树一缩万丈，成了现在那样短小的山芋。

七兄弟无路可归，只好留在天上与玉帝商量。玉帝便叫他们在天上种田，万里碧空就是他们耕作的田地。所以，每当天气晴朗的时候，我们总会见到他们犁过的犁浪——排云或条云。只有七弟不肯和大家在一起，而去给月亮当随从。这就是月亮无论什么时候，都有一颗小星伴行的缘由。而那六兄弟依然像在家一样，团结一致，一起辛勤耕耘着万里云空。这就是络佬②。

## **Brother Constellations**

  Long long ago, there were seven brothers living in a nameless mountain. Although their parents had passed away for a long time, they

---

① 万界：玉帝。
② 络佬：兄弟星座。

got along well with each other and lived a happy life.

They grew Shanlan rice for a living. One year, in order to plant Shanlan rice, the seven brothers cut down trees in the mountain all day. When they were about to chop the sky-high tree named Tianyu tree[①] on the mountainside, it was getting dark, so they packed up their machetes and went home.

The next morning when they came to the mountainside, they found that the trees and thick vines they had cut down the day before grew up again. They wondered but they had to cut down the trees hard for another day. On the third day, when they came to the mountainside, they saw the same thing. All the trees and vines they had cut down the day before grew up once again. They were more confused and wanted to find out the reason. After dark, they did not go home but hid in the woods. In the middle of the night, a bright light flashed in the sky, and then a big pig from the heaven jumped down from the Tianyu tree. The heaven pig puffed out a wisp of white smoke towards the field which had been clear-cut and murmured, "My dear trees, my dear vines, come back again." With these spell, the trees and thick vines that had been cut down revived. After that, the pig jump into the Tianyu tree and returned to the heaven.

The seven brothers decided to kill the heaven pig by using an extremely large bow and a very large arrow, so they built a large bow that could only be pulled by several people and a large arrow with logs. They installed the bow and arrow under the Tianyu tree and vowed that they would go to the heaven to pick with the Jade Emperor after killing the heaven pig.

---

① Tianyu tree: It is said that in ancient times, a sky-high Tianyu tree was a bridge between the heaven and the earth. Later, the youngest brother spilled the soup on the pistil of the tree and it suddenly shrank into a common small yam plant.

On this day, the seven brothers worked together to cut down trees and vines all day long. When it got dark, they hid under the Tianyu tree. Till the midnight, the heaven pig wheezily descended from the Tianyu tree. As soon as the pig puffed out the white smoke, the seven brothers raised the bow and shot it. Whoosh! The pig was shot in the belly. It hurriedly jumped on the stalk of the Tianyu tree and ran straight back to the heaven. The seven brothers shouldered their wooden plough and chased after the pig by following its bloodstains.

The seven brothers arrived in the heaven and found rows of magnificent palaces and pavilions standing in the clouds. They followed the bloodstains to the Jade Emperor's pigsty and saw the huge heaven pig dead there. They made a fuss in the heaven and wanted to get even with the Jade Emperor. Awakened by their noise, the Jade Emperor came to them and asked, "Hey, guys, what are you quarreling about?"

The seven brothers answered plausibly, "His highness, your pig came to the mortal world and ruined the Shanlan rice fields we had reclaimed for several days. We are coming for that!"

The Jade Emperor replied, "Well, since it violated the rules of the heaven and went to the mortal world secretly, and was hunted by you, I will give its body to you. But you must eat it up."

So the seven brothers began to set fire to roast the pig and eat its meat. They ate up the pork with their sharp knives in a short time, but left a gourdful of soup. The youngest brother casually splashed the soup over the pistil of the Tianyu tree. For a moment, the sky-high Tianyu tree turned into a small yam plant. That's the origin of the yam plant.

Without the sky-high Tianyu tree, the seven brothers couldn't find their way back to the human world. They had to stay in the heaven to be arranged by the Jade Emperor. The Jade Emperor asked them to farm in the heaven, and the wide and blue sky was their farmland. Therefore, in sunny days, we can see the waves of the clouds which are farmland ploughed by the brothers. However, as the youngest brother refused to farm there, he served as a servant for the moon. That's why we could often see a small star accompanying the moon. The six brothers farmed hard together in the sky were called Luolao (Brother Constellations).

## 故事八　三套神衣

传说，从前有三个弟兄，自小父母双亡，亲伯亲叔皆无。三兄弟从小就十分勤劳，每日上山砍柴回来换米糊口。有一天，三兄弟又上山去砍柴，到了山上，看见火堆旁坐着一个老婆婆。大哥领着两个弟弟上前问道："老妈妈，你为什么独自坐在这个地方呀？"老人回答说："我无儿无女，只好上山来等死算啦！"三兄弟听了非常同情，还是大哥先说："老妈妈，这样吧，我们兄弟三人父母早亡，您老人家愿意的话，我们认您老人家做妈妈。好么？我们会好好地服侍您老人家的。"老婆婆说："那太好了！"三兄弟砍好柴便领着老婆婆回到他们家里。他们每天上山砍柴，老婆婆煮饭做菜、洗衣服，日子过得十分和睦。

几年后，三兄弟都长大成人了。有一天，老婆婆对他们说："你们都已长大成人了，但还没有娶媳妇。这样吧！我留下三套衣服，如有什么困难就穿上，它会帮助你们的。"说完她就不见了。而留下的三套宝衣，兄弟三人各要了一套，大哥要的是鹰衣，二哥要的是猫衣，三弟要的是鼠衣。后来，大哥和二哥都结了婚，只有三弟是单身汉。

同村有一个奥雅①家里的姑娘叫亚闹，长得很漂亮。有一天，亚闹出门挑水，三弟见了目不转睛地看着她，返家后三天三夜都睡不着觉，一直想法子要把亚闹娶为媳妇。他想来想去也想不出好办法来。一天夜里，他壮着胆子走到亚闹的闺房，敲几声门，轻轻地叫她的名字，可是姑娘不开门。于是他穿起鼠衣，不消一刻时间，

---

① "奥雅"这个称谓原是黎语的音译。"奥"是人，"雅"是老，"奥雅"就是老人的意思。后用来指部族的头人。

他就变成一只老鼠钻进去了。这时，亚闹姑娘突然看见一只老鼠坐在床前的板凳上，便找木棍要打老鼠。只听见老鼠说起话来："亚闹，请不要打我，我是三弟呀！"说罢，他跳下地来，脱下鼠衣，果然是三弟。这时亚闹姑娘和他热情地说起话来，并留他在那里过了一夜。鸡叫三遍，三弟准备回家，却发现他的鼠衣不见了，但他想是姑娘偷偷地藏起来了，不好多问，只好空手而归。

第二天晚上，他想来想去，只好去盗二哥的猫衣了。怎么盗呢？刚好大哥家里杀了一只狗来犒劳帮他砍山兰地的兄弟。在酒席间，他用甜蜜的山兰酒灌醉了二哥和二嫂，便偷偷地取了猫衣去找亚闹姑娘，可是亚闹姑娘还是不开门。他只得又穿上猫衣钻进去，还是坐在那张板凳上"喵喵"直叫。亚闹姑娘看见猫坐在板凳上叫，气恼地说："死猫，叫得烦死我了，我打死你。"这时猫说话了："我不是猫，我是三弟。"他脱掉猫衣对亚闹说："嫁给我吧！我什么办法都有，我们会有好日子过的。"亚闹姑娘又热情地留他过了一夜，又藏起了猫衣。鸡又叫了三遍，三弟又发现猫衣不见了。怎么办呢？他问亚闹，亚闹推说不知道，他又只得空手而归。他又想办法偷来大哥的鹰衣。

一天早上，三弟看到亚闹姑娘打扮得漂漂亮亮地出门，便跟着她。走到半路后，他穿上鹰衣，变成一只老鹰从空中飞下来，抱起亚闹姑娘往山上飞，亚闹吓得哭起来，大喊救命。三弟说："不要怕，我是三弟，你偷了我两件宝衣，我不怪你，只要你嫁给我。"三弟的苦心终于赢得了亚闹姑娘的爱，她答应嫁给他。三弟还不相信，说："如果你假心假意，我就把你放到山上喂蟒蛇。"最后，亚闹姑娘诚心地对天对地发了誓，交出鼠、猫宝衣，并紧紧地抱住了三弟。经过几次周折，他们终于产生了真心的爱，幸福地结了婚。

## Three Magic Costumes

Once upon a time, there were three brothers. Their parents died early and they had no relatives either. They worked very hard every day, cutting fire wood on the mountains to exchange some food to feed themselves. One day, when the three brothers were about to cut woods on the mountainside, they run into an old woman who was sitting by the fire alone. The eldest brother asked, "Old lady, why are you sitting here alone?" The old woman replied, "I have no child to look after me, so I have to come here to wait for death!" The three brothers felt very pity for her. The eldest brother said to her, "Old lady, our parents died early. Would you mind being our mother? We will try our best to look after you." The old woman agreed happily. After cutting the firewood, the three brothers led the old woman back home. Thereafter, while the three brothers were cutting wood in the mountains, the old woman cooked and washed clothes for them. They lived a harmonious life.

A few years later, the three brothers grew up. One day, the old woman said, "Now you have grown up and need to get married. I have three costumes for you. Put the costumes on in case you are in trouble and they will help you." She disappeared after she finished these words and three costumes were left. Each brother got one costume. The eldest brother took the eagle costume, the second brother took the cat costume, and the youngest brother took the rat costume. Later, both the eldest brother and the second brother got married, but the youngest brother was still single.

In the village, there was a beautiful girl from an honorable family called Yanao. One day, when Yanao went out to carry water, the youngest brother saw her and fell in love with her at first sight. For three days and nights he couldn't sleep and kept thinking about how to get Yanao to marry him, but he failed to figure out a good way. One night, he plucked up the courage to go to Yanao's room, knocked at the door and gently called her name, but she did not open the door. So he put his rat costume on and instantly turned into a rat and slipped into the room. When Yanao suddenly saw a rat sitting on the bench in front of the bed, she took a wooden stick to hit it. The rat begged, "Yanao, please don't hit me. I am the third brother!" With these words, he jumped on the ground, took off the rat costume and showed himself. Yanao chatted with him passionately and let him stay overnight. After the rooster crowed three times, the third brother had to leave, but he couldn't find his rat costume. He thought it might had been hidden by Yanao, but it was not easy to ask, so he went back home with empty hands.

On the second night, he had no way out but to steal his second brother's cat costume so as to meet Yanao. It happened that the eldest brother's family held a banquet by killing a dog to treat those who had helped him in slashing the Shanlan field, so the third brother managed to get his second brother and sister-in-law to drink a lot of Shanlan rice wine to make them drunk. Then he secretly took away the cat costume and went to Yanao's room. Yanao didn't open the door, so he put on the cat costume and ducked in, sitting on the bench and meowing. Yanao was very annoyed and yelled, "Damned cat, you are annoying me! I am going to kill you." "I am not a cat. I am the third brother," said the cat. With these words, the third brother took off the cat costume and showed himself. He pleaded, "Marry me, please! I can find ways to make our life happy." Then Yanao let him stay for another night with enthusiasm, and again, hid the cat costume. When the rooster crowed the third time, the third brother had to leave, but he couldn't find the cat costume. Of course Yanao said she didn't know anything about it. He had to go back home with empty hands again. Later, he managed to get the eagle costume from his eldest brother.

One morning, when the third brother saw Yanao dressed up beautifully and went out, he secretly followed her to a secluded place. He put on the eagle costume, turned into an eagle, flew up in the sky, and picked up Yanao to the mountain top. Yanao was so scared that she cried and shouted for help. The third brother said, "Don't be afraid. I am the third brother. You stole my two magic costumes. I don't blame you as long as you marry me." Yanao was touched by him and promised to marry him, but the third brother did not believe her this time. He vowed, "I will put you on the mountain top to feed the python if I find you lying." Finally, Yanao vowed to the heaven and the earth, and promised to be sincere to him. She then returned the rat costume and cat costume to him, and hugged him tightly. Finally, they fell in love with each other and got married happily.

## 故事九 陵水县县名的由来

《正德琼台志》载：唐武德五年（622），始置陵水县。故"陵水"一名已有1000多年的历史了。关于"陵水"一名的由来，民间有一个动人的传说。

古时候，陵水原名"灵水"，因有一口井能检验人的品德优劣、操行高下而得名。不论皇孙公侯、平民百姓，不论职位高低、工种殊异，只要靠近这眼井，是品行优良的，井水就呈现澄清透明；是品行低下的，井水就呈现污秽浑浊。老百姓皆称这口井为"灵水"。那些贪官污吏、阿谀之辈、不端之徒，都恶而远之。但老百姓因此也知道，不敢靠近灵水的人，不是什么好东西。后来，一天夜里，贪官主使，污吏督阵，狗腿们把灵水填了个严严实实。沧海桑田，时过境迁，灵水井踪迹已无从寻觅，只留县名和传说在人间。

"陵水"之"灵"自然不可信，但灵水的传说，体现了人民群众要求考核官吏、奖罚得当的愿望。

## The Origin of the Name of Lingshui County

According to *Qiongtai Chorography of the Zhengde Period*, Lingshui county was founded in the fifth year of the reign of Emperor Wude of the Tang Dynasty (622 A. D.). Therefore, the name of "Lingshui" has a history of over 1000 years. Its origin is connected with a touching folklore.

In ancient times, Lingshui was formerly known as magic water because there was a well which was able to test a person's morality and conduct and evaluate him/her as good or bad no matter who he/she was or what his/her position and profession was. As long as a man with good character got close to the well, the water in the well would turn clear and transparent; otherwise, the water would be murky. Therefore, people called the well magic water. Those corrupt officials, flatterers and villains were so afraid of the well that they dared not approach it. Consequently, people realized that those who dared not approach the well were not good people. Later, under the command of the corrupt officials, their henchmen filled the well overnight. As time went by, trace of the well could not be found, just leaving the name and a folktale in the world.

The magic power of Lingshui was unbelievable, but the folktale of the magic water reflected people's desire to valuate officials' performance as well as reward and punish them properly.

## 故事十　马伏波与白马井

在乐东县的尖峰岭下，有一块宽平的大石块，石块上有一双清晰的马蹄印。离它数一里①远的河滩上又有一口水清如镜的白马井。

相传光武帝时，伏波将军马援被派南征。伏波将军乘骑白马，身披盔甲，日夜兼程，率军浩浩荡荡南来。他武艺超群，威震南疆。当他驰马来到尖峰岭下时，仰望高高的山峰，被它挡住了去路。他策马跳上一块大石，使尽浑身力气，拉满弓弦，对准尖峰岭的顶峰射去。别看箭小弓轻，却有万钧之力，箭头所及，只见尖峰岭的顶峰横断一角。因伏波将军射箭用力，马蹄入石三分，留下了深深的蹄印。那蹄印至今尚存，尖峰岭顶也因此不尖。

伏波将军射断尖峰之后，马不停蹄，翻山越岭，勇往直前。飞马来到感恩县的沙滩地带时，日正当午，烈日笼笼，人马都渴得不可开交。白马临渴挖井，它用前蹄往下猛挖，挖呀挖呀，终于挖出了一个深洞，清清的泉水直冒，马欢人笑，皆大欢喜。他们痛饮清泉，清甜透肺，精神倍增，胜利班师回朝。事后，人们便把白马挖出来的深洞围筑成井，称为"白马井"，又名"马伏波井"。

## General Fubo and the White Horse Well

Under the Jianfengling Mountain (Jianfeng means sharp peak) of Ledong County, there is a huge flat stone with a pair of hoof prints on it. Miles away from the stone, there is a river. And on the beach of the river there is a spring called Baimajing (white horse well), whose water

---

① 1 里 = 500 米。

surface is as clear as a mirror.

According to legend, during the reign of the Emperor Guangwu in the Han Dynasty, General Ma Yuan (with the title of General Fubo) was sent to pacify the south. Wearing armor and riding a white horse, he led the army southward day and night. Due to his outstanding military skill, he was well known in the south area. When the army reached the foot of the Jianfengling Mountain, the high mountain blocked their way. He rode the horse jumping on a huge stone, exerted all his energies and drew his bow to shoot at the peak of the Jianfengling Mountain. His arrow was so powerful that the peak was cut down. As he used too much energy, the horse he rode pressed its hooves deeply into the stone. Till now, you can clearly see the hoof prints on the stone and since then the ever sharp peak of Jianfengling Mountain has not been so sharp.

After that, he commanded the army to climb the mountains without a single halt. When they came to the beach of Gan'en County at noon, the sun was so hot that both soldiers and horses were thirsty to death. The white horse couldn't bear the thirst and began to dig the ground with its front hoofs. It dug and dug and finally dug out a deep hole with water in it. When the clear water welled up, they were very happy. After drinking the sweet and clear spring water, both soldiers and horses were energetic again. As a result, they achieved victory effortlessly. After the army left, the local people turn the deep hole into a well and called it Baimajing or Ma Fubo Well.

## 故事十一　冼夫人解救俚女

梁朝大同年间，海南归附冼夫人之后，冼夫人请求朝廷建置崖州，并派她家族中得力的人到海南岛做官。岛上各地的俚人从此开始过上了比较安定的日子。

广州有一个姓欧阳的大官，是一个又凶残又好色、贪得无厌的家伙。他娶了大妻小妾共九个，但一见到漂亮的姑娘仍不肯放过，使得有姑娘的人家一听说他路过就不敢开门。他的家族从他的父辈开始就统治岭南的十几个州，但他连这些州的名称都记不清，听说建立了崖州，他又想把崖州也纳入他的地盘。

有一年，冼夫人到海南巡视，那个欧阳大官也赶紧跟踪而来，所到之处，为非作歹，无恶不作。一次，欧阳一伙正在赶路，突然看见路边小山包上有一位少女正在种山兰稻，他立即下令停步，派几个亲兵去把那位少女叫来。

少女一看见官兵，拔腿就跑，但跑不过他们，不一会儿，几个亲兵就连拖带抬，把少女抓过来了。欧阳这个老色鬼，远远看见那位少女的美貌，心里就发痒。

奴才最知主子的心意，那几个亲兵连吓带诱，将少女推到马背上。欧阳吩咐马上打道回府，即日启程离琼返粤。

正在这时，远处传来哒哒的马蹄声，尘土滚处，奔过来一队娘子军。欧阳一看这阵势，心里就有点慌张起来。他猜到来的一定是冼夫人，因此，心里暗暗做好对付的准备。

欧阳果然猜对了——来的正是冼夫人。双方行过见面礼后，欧阳就想赶快溜。哪知冼夫人眼尖，一眼就看到坐在马背上的少女。冼夫人问："请问大人，为何要捆绑这少女？"

"唔……这个你也要管么？"欧阳反问。

71

冼夫人昂头说:"当然要管,珠崖父老尊我为圣母,就是希望我像保护自己的孩子一样保护他们的儿女。"

"不过,我也劝你别扫了老子的兴,老子不是好惹的!"欧阳的语气更加厉害。

冼夫人也不示弱:"我也劝大人一句,珠崖俚民也不是好惹的!"

欧阳无语。冼夫人接着说:"大人妻妾成群,奴婢满屋,何必计较一个小姑娘,伤了珠崖俚人的感情。"

欧阳气得正要发火,突然,他的军师凑近身边,在他耳旁嘀咕了几句,劝欧阳大官别吃眼前亏,避过锋芒,日后再想办法来抓这个少女。欧阳那双贼眼转了几转,点了点头。他来了一个一百八十度的态度转变,竖起拇指,哈哈大笑地说:"冼夫人果然名不虚传。本官今天就依军师的,将姑娘交给你,让你做个人情。"说完,命令亲兵放下少女,溜走了。

那位少女谢过冼夫人的救命之恩,一定要跟随娘子军。冼夫人知道欧阳不会轻易放过少女,为了保护这位民女,便答应了她的请求。

果然,阴险毒辣的欧阳一伙自以为得计,他们趁着冼夫人已离开这里,又折回来骚扰这一带的村峒,企图再抢走那个少女。抓空后,又赶回广州策划报复冼夫人。

## Madam Xian Rescuing a Native Girl

During the years of Datong in the Liang Dynasty, Hainan was under the government of Madam Xian. She requested the imperial court to establish Yazhou Prefecture in Hainan, and sent her competent relatives to rule there. Since then, people on the island have begun to live a steady life.

A senior officer named Ouyang in Guangzhou was fierce, lascivious and greedy. Although he had nine wives and concubines at home, he would abduct other beautiful girls and force them to be his concubines whenever he had a chance. So the families with girls were afraid to open their doors when they heard Ouyang was passing by. The Ouyang family had ruled more than a dozen prefectures in Lingnan area since his elder generation, but he even couldn't remember the names of these prefectures. As soon as he heard that Yazhou Prefecture was established, he wanted to control it.

One year, Madam Xian went to Hainan for inspecting, and Ouyang followed her. Wherever he reached, he committed all sorts of crimes. One day, when Ouyang was on his way with his henchmen and saw a girl planting Shanlan rice on the hill, he immediately ordered a stop and sent several soldiers to call the girl.

As soon as the girl saw the soldiers, she began to flee, but was caught in a while and dragged to Ouyang. Ouyang was immediately excited by the girl's beauty and wanted to deforce her.

Ouyang's henchmen knew his intention very well, so they intimidated and tempted the girl to get on the horseback. Then Ouyang was ready to take the girl back to Guangzhou immediately.

At that moment, the clip-clop of horses' hooves came from afar, and with rolling dust, a team of female soldiers were coming over. Ouyang knew Madam Xian was coming, he felt a little nervous and tried to find ways to deal with her.

Ouyang was right — it was Madam Xian. After saluted to each other, Ouyang wanted to leave quickly. Madame Xian had sharp eyes and saw the girl sitting on horseback at a glance. She asked, "Excuse me, Mr. Ouyang, why do you tie up this girl?"

"Alright, do you have to meddle in it?" Ouyang asked.

Madam Xian said with her head high, "Of course, Yazhou people respect me as their patron goddess, and they hope I can protect their children just like protecting mine."

"Okay, but I also suggest you do not spoil my fun. I am not the one to be trifled with!" Ouyang's tone was even harsher.

Madam Xian replied with no fear, "I also suggest you, Sir. Yazhou people are not afraid of getting into any trouble!"

Ouyang was speechless. Madam Xian continued, "Mr. Ouyang, you have a houseful of wives and concubines. Why do you care about a little girl and hurt the feelings of the Yazhou people?"

Ouyang became very angry and was about to lose his temper. Suddenly his counselor approached his ear and said a few words secretly. He advised Ouyang not to fight when the odds were against him, and temporary avoidance of contradiction would lead another chance to find ways to catch the girl. Ouyang moved his shifty eyes from side to side and agreed. He came to a dramatic change, raised his thumb, and laughed, "Madam Xian really well deserves the reputation. Alright, I'll follow my counselor's words and leave the girl to you as a special favor." Then, he ordered his followers to lay down the girl and left.

The girl thanked Madam Xian for saving her life, and begged to join the women army. Knowing that Ouyang would not easily give up and in order to protect the girl, Madam Xian agreed to her request.

Unsurprisingly, the treacherous gang of Ouyang returned. They thought that Madam Xian should have left and their plan should have been successful, so they harassed the villages in the area in an attempt to catch the girl again, but they failed. After that, Ouyang rushed back to Guangzhou to plan to retaliate against Madam Xian.

## 故事十二　纺织女神黄道婆

黄道婆是宋末元初我国一位杰出的女纺织革新家。传说她出生于崖州北厢一个贫穷的农民家庭，自幼父母双亡，孤苦伶仃，经常给人家放牛过日子。

黄道婆在十六岁那年嫁给西厢宋家的第五个儿子宋老五，邻居称她宋五娘。黄道婆婚后两年都没有生养孩子，经常受到公婆的责骂和旁人的白眼。几年后，宋老五不幸病亡，她的日子更难过了。公婆打骂她，旁人讥笑她，她忍受不了，被迫离家出走，流落到西界的透风村，在一户人家里学习纺纱织布。后来这家人知道她是个寡妇，怕沾上衰气，便冷言冷语叫她走。她返回婆家，但婆婆不准她进家门。她走投无路，被迫出家到广度寺当尼姑。广度寺在西关村旁，离婆家不远，婆家的闲言闲语不断传到她的耳中，她一刻也不得清净和安宁，在广度寺也待不下去了。

这天，她离开了广度寺，不知不觉来到了南山岭脚下的南山村。这是一个黎村，村子周围长着一片片木棉树，家家户户都有纺车和织机，比透风村的齐全且好得多。南山村黎族妇女的手工很好，人人善于纺织刺绣，织出的裙、被服非常好看，纱线细密，花纹美丽，颜色鲜艳。她看在眼里，想在心上：只要学好一门手艺就谁也不怕了。她在南山村住了下来，拜一位黎族妇女为师，日夜跟她学习纺纱、织布、绣花。黄道婆心灵手巧，很快就学会了黎族的纺织手艺。她还和这位黎族女师傅一起将单线纺车改为双线纺车，后再改为三线纺车。同时，她还设计绘制了新的刺绣装饰花图案，调配颜色。黄道婆和黎族妇女们织的布和刺绣品在汉区很抢手。后来，黎族的纺织工具和手艺还传到了崖州各个汉区。黎族人民更加喜欢黄道婆了，把她当亲姐妹一样看待。

黄道婆在黎寨生活了三十年,一直不入州城。她五十多岁那年,不知道出于什么原因,乘坐一艘商船从崖州湾的大蛋港离开崖州去了大陆,住在松江越彩石。她将黎族的纺织技术传授给那里的人们,并改革了纺织工具,上海纺织业很快发展起来了。黄道婆的名字和事迹也传回了崖州。

黄道婆死后,越彩石人民建了庙堂纪念她,崖州人民修建了宋五娘庙(今崖城镇农业技术推广站)。

# Huang Daopo, the Goddess of Textiles

Huang Daopo was an outstanding female textile innovator in the late Song Dynasty and early Yuan Dynasty. Legend has it that she was born in a poor peasant family in the northern region of Yazhou. Her parents died at her early age and left her alone, so she used to make a living by herding cattle for others.

When Huang was sixteen years old, she married the fifth son of the Song family in the western region and was called Song Wuniang by her neighbors. After two years, Huang did not give birth to any child, so she was often scolded by her parents-in-law and looked down upon by others. Years later, her husband died of illness, and her life was even worse. Her parents-in-law beat and scolded her, and others laughed at her. She could not bear it and left home. She wandered to Toufeng Village in the west region and began to learn to spin and weave in a family. But later when the family knew she was a widow, for fear of being infected with bad luck, they began to sneer at her and asked her to leave. She had to return to her in-laws' home, but her mother-in-law forbade her to enter the house. She was desperate and had no choice but to become a nun in Guangdu Temple. Guangdu Temple was near Xiguan Village, not far from her in-laws' home. The gossip from her in-laws' family kept spreading to her ears, so she couldn't stay at Guangdu Temple any more.

One day, she left Guangdu Temple and came to Nanshan Village at the foot of the Nanshan Mountain unconsciously. Surrounded by kapok trees, this village was the residence of the Li people. Every household had spinning wheels and looms, which were much better than those of the Han nationality in Toufeng Village. The handicraft of the Li women in Nanshan Village was very good. Everyone was good at textile and embroidery. The skirts and quilts woven were very beautiful. The yarns were fine, the patterns were beautiful and the colors were bright. She thought that she would be afraid of no one as long as she learned the skills well, so she settled down in Nanshan Village. There she studied spinning, weaving and embroidery from a Li woman day and night. Huang was very clever and learned Li people's textile skills quickly. Together with the Li woman tutor, she changed the single-thread spinning wheel into the double-thread spinning wheel, and then to the three-thread spinning wheel, which improved the spinning speed. At the same time, she designed new embroidery decorative patterns and mixed different colors into new ones. The cloth and embroidery woven by Huang and the Li women were very popular in the Han districts. The textile tools and crafts of the Li nationality were later introduced to various Han districts in Yazhou. The Li people liked Huang even better and treated her as their sister.

Huang Daopo lived in the Li village for 30 years and never went to the prefectural city. When she was in her fifties, for an unknown reason, she left Yazhou for the mainland by a merchant ship from Dadan Port in Yazhou Bay. Then she lived in Yuecaishi of Songjiang (Shanghai). She passed on the textile technology of the Li nationality to the people there and reformed the textile tools, which helped the development of the textile industry in Shanghai. Later, Huang Daopo's name and deeds were spread to Yazhou.

After her death, people of Yuecaishi built a temple to commemorate her, and the people of Yazhou also built the Song Wuniang Temple (now the Agricultural Technology Station of Yacheng Town) to memorize her.

# 故事十三　五指山的传说

传说很久以前,海南岛上并没有五指山。那里原来是一片大平原。在这块平原上,居住着一对夫妇,丈夫名叫阿力,妻子名叫哪迈。他们生有五个孩子。一家人虽然日夜辛勤劳动,但由于没有锄头,没有砍刀,好几天砍不了一小块山,种植的坡稻数量很少,始终无法填饱肚子。

一天夜里,哪迈和孩子们都熟睡了,只有阿力翻来覆去睡不着,想着如何把荒地开得更多一些,让全家人填饱肚子。可是他想呀,想呀,想了半夜,依然想不出个好主意来。深夜,他昏昏沉沉睡去,忽然梦见一个白胡须老人站在床前,说:"在你们家附近有一把宝锄和宝剑,你们挖出来使用吧。只要你高高举起那把宝锄叫一声'挖',平原上的荒地就会变成良田;你挥舞一下那把宝剑叫一声'砍',大树就会应声倒地;要是坏人来侵犯,只要你喊一声'杀',坏人就会人头落地。"

清早,阿力把梦中老人的话告诉家人,大家听了很兴奋,一齐动手用木棍在茅屋四周挖了起来。挖呀,刨呀,他们从早上挖到太阳落山。忽然,阿力"哎哟"叫了一声,从土里刨出一把黑油油的宝锄和一把闪光发亮的宝剑。阿力按照白胡须老人的话,挥舞宝剑并叫了一声"砍",顿时一阵巨响,房屋周围的许多大树野藤一齐应声倒地。哪迈高举宝锄,叫了一声"挖",荒地果然变成一片片良田。从此,阿力一家人生活过得很美满。

一晃就是七十年。老阿力临死的时候,把五个孩子叫到眼前说,荒地已经开得不少了,嘱咐他们小心种好作物,宝锄和宝剑要交还白胡须老人,让他转送给没有田地的穷人。话刚说完,阿力就合上眼睛死了。埋葬父亲的时候,五个儿子依照他的遗嘱,把宝锄和宝剑作为陪葬品，同时埋到墓里去。

阿力的死讯传到坏人阿尾的耳里，他勾结海盗，派来几百人，抢占了这块肥沃美丽的土地。他们杀死了哪迈，把她五个儿子也同时捉了起来，狠心的阿尾用红藤绑着阿力的五个儿子，审问拷打了十天十夜，逼他们交出宝锄和宝剑。五兄弟个个被打得遍体鳞伤，但始终不肯说出埋葬宝锄和宝剑的地方。阿尾发怒了，用火烧他们。五个兄弟流下来的汗水和眼泪把平原冲成五条溪，他们死去的时候，四面八方的熊、豹、山猪、蚂蚁、黄蜂、山鹰成群结队地赶来，把阿尾和海盗统统咬死，并搬来许多泥土和大石块，把五兄弟的尸体埋住，筑成了五座高高的山。人们为了纪念死去的阿力和哪迈的五个儿子，就把这五座山叫作"五子山"。后来，人们看到五子山好像五只手指，便改称为"五指山"。

# The Legend of the Wuzhishan Mountain

Long ago there was no Wuzhishan Mountain on Hainan Island, and there used to be a great plain. On the plain lived a couple, the husband named Ali and the wife named Namai. They had five children. Although the family worked hard day and night, they still couldn't cultivate a small hill for several days as they didn't have hoes and machetes. The amount of rice they planted was so small that they could not fill their stomachs.

One night, while Namai and the children were sleeping soundly, Ali could not sleep. He was thinking about how to cultivate more wasteland and let the whole family fill their stomachs. He thought about it over and over again till midnight, but still couldn't come up with a good idea. Late at night, he fell asleep and dreamed an old man with white beard standing by his bed. The old man said, "A treasured hoe and a sword were near your house. Dig them out and use them. Raise the hoe and shout 'dig', then the wasteland on the plain will become good field;

wave the sword and shout 'cut', then the trees will fall to the ground; if bad men invade, just shout 'kill' and they will be killed."

Early the next morning, Ali told his family what he had dreamed of. Everyone was very excited and they began to dig around the hut with sticks. They kept digging from morning till sunset. Suddenly, with the sound of cling-clang, Ali dug out a pitch-dark hoe and a shining sword from the soil. Following the words of the old man with white beard, Ali waved the sword and shouted "cut". With a loud noise, big trees and wild vines around the house fell to the ground immediately. Then Namai held the treasured hoe up high and shouted "dig", and the land immediately turned into good field. From then on, the family lived a happy life.

Seventy years passed in a flash. When old Ali was dying, he called his five sons to his bed and said that the fertile land was enough for them and they should grow crops carefully. The hoe and sword should be returned to the old man with white beard so that he could transfer them to the poor without land. As soon as he finished these words, Ali closed his eyes and died. The five sons buried the hoe and sword along with their father in the tomb according to their father's will.

The news of Ali's death reached the ears of Awei the villain. He colluded with the pirates to send hundreds of villains to seize the fertile land. They killed Namai and caught her five sons. Awei tied Ali's five sons with red vines and tortured them for ten days and nights, forcing them to surrender their hoe and sword. The five brothers were beaten all over, but they refused to tell where the hoe and sword were buried. Awei was angry and burned them with fire. The sweat and tears shed from the five brothers turned the plains into five streams. At that moment, bears, leopards, boars, ants, hornets, and mountain eagles came in droves and killed Awei and the pirates. They moved a large amount of dirt and big stones to bury the bodies of the five brothers, which turned into five high mountains. In memory of the five sons of Ali and Namai, the five mountains were called the Wuzishan Mountain (Five-son Mountain). Later, when people saw that Wuzishan Mountain looked like five fingers, they changed the name into the Wuzhishan Mountain (Five-finger Mountain).

## 故事十四　七仙岭

雄伟美丽的七仙岭,传说是由杞黎的祖先从大海里把石头赶来堆成的。

据说很久很久以前,三弓峒有个叫楠的杞黎老大爷,夫妇俩很勤劳,一生开了很多梯田,种了不少槟榔、椰子,还养了一群牛,生活过得很富裕。可是年已过半百,还没有养育孩子,夫妇俩为此事感到很苦恼。

有一个晚上,楠的老伴范梦见两颗明亮的星星掉进她的怀里就不见了。她到处寻找,怎么也找不到,醒后发现原来是一场梦。就在那一年里,她一胎就生了两个儿子,夫妻俩那高兴劲就不用提了。儿子刚满月,楠就办了酒席,请乡亲们都来高兴高兴。他给儿子起了名字,老大叫那跃,老二叫那扎差。

那跃和那扎差长得很快。兄弟俩到七岁时,楠就带他们去打猎,范也常常带他们下地干活。父母常对他们说谁勤劳又诚实,将来就由谁管家里的财产。

时间过得真快,转眼间兄弟俩都成青年人了。哥哥那跃个子很高,而弟弟那扎差却是个矮子。兄弟俩臂力过人,能射一手好箭。只要进山打猎,谁都不会空手回来,不是打到熊、豹,便是山猪、野鹿。乐得老两口整天笑呵呵的。

有一天,楠把两个儿子都叫到跟前,对他们说:"你们谁能到大海去抓点鱼回来呢?"兄弟俩都说能,争着要下海去抓鱼。楠笑着说:"那很好,你们都去,看谁干得好。"

第二天,天刚蒙蒙亮,兄弟俩就起程去大海抓鱼。那跃个子高,步子大;那扎差虽然是个矮子,但步子跨得快,所以都同时到达海滨。刚好海滨有个叫作尚的城市,做买卖的人很多,花花绿绿的。那扎差被那里的景象迷住了,看呀看呀,哥哥叫他也听不见,把抓鱼的事都忘了。但那跃不管那些,在城里吃完饭就下海去抓鱼。天刚过午,他便捉到一担鲜鱼了。他叫呀找呀,怎么也见不到那扎差。实在没办法,他就自己回家了。老两口见那跃挑鱼回来,很高兴,他们做了一顿丰盛的晚餐。

时间很晚了,那扎差才提着一些小鱼虾回来。楠问他为什么才抓到这么一点鱼,那扎差说海里的鱼很少,幸好他努力才捉到这么一点。

楠又问:"你哥哥为什么捉到那么多呢?"

那扎差看到哥哥捉了一担鱼,再也没话好说了。

楠又对兄弟俩说:"离我们这里不远的地方,有座风门岭,年年大风都从那里吹来,把我们的房子和庄稼都吹跑了。我想在我们周围筑起大岭,挡住大风,你们看怎么样?"

那跃说:"我也这么想,我明天就动手。"

那扎差说:"要筑能挡风的岭,有那么容易吗?"

那跃说:"当然不那么容易,但只要有决心,一定能办到。"

楠说:"那跃说得对。只要有决心和恒心,什么事都能办到。"

那扎差看见楠也站在那跃一边说话,也只好同意了。

说干就干,第二天,兄弟俩就开始造岭了。那跃在东面,那扎差在西边。

只见东面灰尘滚滚遮了半边天,原来是那跃用鞭子催赶一堆海里的大石头以在那里造岭。不久,他便用石头堆起了比风门岭还高的大石岭。那扎差见哥哥造的岭已经成了,也日夜赶工,西边的大岭也造成了。他自己取了个名字叫铁岭。

楠看了兄弟俩造的岭后说:"你们俩谁造的岭结实?"

那扎差说:"我造的岭叫铁岭,当然结实。"

那跃说:"我造的是石头岭,是否结实请父亲检验。"

楠说:"不用我检验,你俩的箭威力不是很大吗?就让那跃射铁岭,那扎差射石头岭,你们看怎么样?"

那跃高兴地说:"那就让弟弟先射吧。"

那扎差二话不说,站好架势,用力拉满牛角弓,"嗖"的一声,石头岭上发出雷鸣般的巨响,只见石头岭裂了一条缝。"嗖、嗖、嗖"连射了六箭,石头岭连裂六条缝,把石头岭分成七座石头峰了。楠看了说:"好,很结实,这座石头岭就叫七峰岭吧。"后来人们把七峰岭叫作七仙岭。现在七仙岭上的石头都有用鞭子抽打过的痕迹,那是那跃在赶石头时打的。

那扎差射完,那跃才弯弓搭箭,"嗖"的一声,西边铁岭上轰隆一声巨响,好像山崩地裂,铁岭被削去半截。

楠说:"别射了,再射西面就没有岭啦。"

他们走到铁岭一看,原来岭都是用泥土堆成的。被箭削去的岭顶,中间还有一个看不到底的洞。啊,岭是空心的呀!楠说:"这座岭被箭削后形状像砧板,就叫铁砧岭好了。"

那扎差见自己造的铁岭有名无实,羞得没脸见人,赶快钻进岭上的无底洞里去了。他一辈子再也没有出来过。后来人们又把这座铁砧岭改名叫平顶山。山顶上那口洞现在还在呢。

不久,楠老两口先后去世,家业就由那跃接管了。据说,杞黎就是那跃的后代,既勤劳,又诚实。

# The Legend of Qixianling Ridge

The magnificent and beautiful Qixianling Ridge is said to have been built by the ancestors of the Qili ethnic group with stones they drove from the sea.

According to legend, a long time ago, there was an old man in the Qili ethnic group named Nan in Sangong Village. Nan and his wife worked very hard. They cultivated many terraced fields, planted lots of betel nuts and coconuts, and raised a herd of cattle. They lived a rich life. However, although they were over 50 years old, they didn't have any child, which upset them very much.

One night, Nan's wife Fan dreamed of two bright stars falling into her arms and disappearing, then she looked everywhere, but could not find them. When she woke up, she realized that it was a dream. Later that year, she gave birth to twin brothers, and the couple was very happy. As soon as the sons were one month old, Nan held a banquet and invited villagers to celebrate. He named the twin brothers Nayue the elder and Nazhacha the younger.

Nayue and Nazacha grew very fast. When the brothers were seven years old, Nan began to take them to hunt and Fan also took them to the field to work. The parents often told them that whoever was diligent and honest would be in charge of the family's property in the future.

Time flied so quickly that in a blink of an eye both brothers became young men. Nayue was very tall, while Nazhacha was short. The two brothers have great strength and could shoot arrows very well. Whenever they went hunting in mountains, neither of them would come back empty-handed. They often hunted bear, leopard, boar or deer, which satisfied the old couple.

One day Nan called both sons to him and asked, "Who can go to the sea and catch some fish back?" Both brothers said that they could catch fish. Nan replied with a smile, "That's good. You both go and let's see who can catch more fish."

The next morning, just before dawn, the twin brothers set out to the sea to catch fish. Nayue was taller and his steps were bigger. Nazhacha was shorter, but his pace was faster. They both reached the beach at the same time. It happened that there was a city called Shang on the seashore. Many people were doing business and the street was very lively. Nazhacha was fascinated by the scenery there, so he looked at this and that, wandered here and there, forgetting the mission of catching fish. He even couldn't hear his brother's calling. Nayue didn't care about the scenery and went to the sea to catch fish after breakfast. It was just at noon that he caught a load of fresh fish. He looked for Nazhacha but failed to find him, so he had to return home alone. Seeing Nayue came back with a lot of fish, the old couple was very satisfied and made a big dinner.

It was very late, and Nazhacha came back with some small fish and shrimps. Nan asked him why he only caught a few fish. Nazhacha said that there were not so many fish in the sea. Fortunately, he worked hard to catch some.

"Why did your brother catch so many?" Asked Nan.

Nazarcha saw that his brother had caught a load of fish so he had nothing to say.

Nan said to the twin brothers, "Not far from us, there is a Wind-gate Ridge. Every year the strong wind blows from there, blowing away our houses and crops. I want you to build a big ridge around us to keep out of the strong wind. How do you think?"

Nayue replied, "I think so too. I'll start tomorrow."

Nazhacha replied, "Is it so easy to build a windbreak ridge?"

Nayue said, "Of course, it's not easy, but as long as we have the determination, we can do it."

Nan nodded, "Nayue is right. Anything can be done with determination and perseverance."

Nazhacha saw Nan standing on Nayue's side so he had to agree.

The next day, both brothers began to build ridges. Nayue built from the east side and Nazhacha from the west.

The dust in the east covered half of the sky. It turned out that the huge rocks in the sea were driven by Nayue's whips to build ridge there. Soon, a huge stone ridge which was higher than the Wind-gate Ridge was heaped up with stones. When Nazhacha saw that his brother's ridge had been built, he began to build his ridge day and night, and finally the western ridge was completed. He named it Iron Ridge.

Nan looked at the ridges built by the twin brothers and asked, "Which ridge is much stronger?"

Nazhacha answered, "The ridge I built is called Iron Ridge. Of course it is stronger."

Nayue said, "What I built is a stone ridge. Father can check whether it is strong or not."

Nan replied, "I don't need to check. Why not use those powerful arrows of yours to check them? Nayue shoot at the Iron Ridge and Nazhacha shoot at the stone ridge. Do you agree?"

Nayue said happily, "Let my younger brother shoot first."

Nazhacha did not say a word. He stood in a good posture, drew his horn bow with full strength and let it go. The arrow swished and flew to the ridge and made a thunderous noise on the stone, only to see a crack in the stone ridge. Six arrows were shot and six cracks were made in the stone ridge, which were divided into seven stone peaks. Nan looked at it and said, "Well, it's very strong. Let's call the stone ridge Qifengling Ridge (Seven-peak Ridge)." Later, people called it Qixianling Ridge. Now all the stones on Qixianling Ridge have traces of being beaten with whips, which were left by Nayue when he drove the stones.

After Nazhacha had finished shooting, Nayue began to shoot. With a loud noise, the landslide and crack happened in the Iron Ridge, and the ridge was cut in half.

Nan said, "Stop shooting, or there will be no ridge in the west."

When they came nearer, they found that the ridge was made of mud. At the top of the ridge cut by the arrow, there was a hole in the middle in which no body could see the bottom. It turned out to be a hollow ridge! Nan said, "Now that the ridge is like an anvil, let's call it Iron Anvil Ridge."

Nazhacha was so ashamed of the ridge he had built that he quickly ducked into the bottomless cave and had never come out since then. Later, people renamed the Iron Anvil Ridge as Flat-top Mountain. Till now, the cave on the top of the hill is still there.

Soon after, the old couple died one after another, and Nayue took over the family business. It is said that the Qili people are the descendants of Nayue who are both diligent and honest.

## 故事十五　鹿回头村

从前,马岭的黎寨里有一位年轻人,名叫阿贺。他诚实善良,勤劳勇敢,以打猎为生,是一位远近闻名的猎手。

有一次,阿贺又到深山里打猎,巡了两天两夜,一只禽兽的影子也不见。第三天早上,他已经不知不觉地来到了龙楼山。他感到又饥又渴,就在山边摘了些野果,来到一条河的河边吃。

阿贺嚼着野果,饮着河水,忽然听到三声呦呦的鹿鸣。他寻声抬头一看,一只小鹿正在河西岸向他张望。这小鹿毛色光鲜,身上长着红色的斑纹。阿贺打了十年猎,从未见过这样美丽的山鹿。他高兴极了,拔出箭来,随即却又插回袋中。这只山鹿太可爱了,他不忍心射杀它,决心活捉它回家养。

红花鹿不怕人,它看着阿贺奔到跟前,鸣叫一声,才不紧不慢地走进山里。阿贺赶紧追上去,红花鹿却转身向西南方向跑。阿贺紧追不放。一路上,红花鹿像是跟阿贺开玩笑做游戏,有好几次,它见阿贺追不上,慢慢走着等,阿贺追上来,眼看伸手就捉着,它却一跃就跃出十丈八丈远,惹得阿贺很气愤。

红花鹿逗引着阿贺到了南海边,阿贺咬咬牙,拔出箭,瞄准红花鹿一箭射去。箭支飞上了天空。他又射出第二箭,箭却又飞下大海。连续射了八箭,支支都落空。他拔出最后的第九支箭,慢慢地靠近红花鹿,搭上箭,拉满弓,正要放手射出时,红花鹿忽地长鸣一声,回过头来,慢慢地朝他走来,走着走着,变成一位美丽的姑娘。阿贺愣住了,他又惊又喜。这姑娘害羞带笑地走来,右手搭在阿贺肩上,轻轻地摇,轻轻地唱:

"阿哥好仪表,

侬想把心交,

阿哥有胆量，

做吃肯耐劳。"

阿贺不好意思地问：

"妹从哪里来？

肉菜①如此好？

此样好容貌，

做乜来相找？"

鹿姑娘脸一红，低下头来答道：

"五指山神女，

小名叫阿娇，

阿哥要吃水，

妹愿做水瓢。"

阿贺像喝了三碗山兰酒，醉了。他攀扶着鹿姑娘的腰肢，唱道：

"妹歌似天调，

靓过鹦哥鸟，

今日捡得宝，

木棉开花苞。"

鹿姑娘也像醉了的槟榔一样，脸更红了。她把头埋在阿贺的怀里，悄声唱道：

"阿哥人枯燥，

孤单静悄悄，

夜给哥铺席，

日替哥守寮。"

阿贺忍不住，把鹿姑娘搂过来抱在怀里。

阿贺和鹿姑娘后来生了两男两女，子娶老婆，女儿招郎家，儿孙后代在那里生活，成了大村庄。后来，人们就把这村子叫作鹿回

---

① 指身体丰满健康。

头村。

## Luhuitou Village

Once upon a time, there was a young man named Ahe in the Li stockaded village of Maling Mountain. He was honest, kind, hard-working and brave. He made a living by hunting and was a well-known hunter far and near.

One day, Ahe went hunting in the deep mountains. He toured for two days and nights, without finding the shadow of an animal. In the third morning, he came to Longloushan Mountain unconsciously. Feeling hungry and thirsty, he picked some wild fruit by the mountainside and came to a river bank to eat.

As he was chewing wild fruit and drinking the river water, he suddenly heard three loud bleats of a deer. He looked up and saw a deer looking at him on the west bank. The deer had bright fur with red markings. Ahe had hunted for ten years but had never seen such a beautiful deer. He was very happy and pulled out an arrow from the quiver, but he put it back immediately. The deer was so cute that he could not bear to shoot at it. He decided to catch it alive and take it home.

The deer was not afraid of him. When it saw Ahe rushing near, it gave a bleat and run slowly into the mountain. Ahe ran after it, and the deer turned southwest. Ahe kept on chasing. Along the way, the deer seemed to play a joke with Ahe. For several times, when it saw that Ahe couldn't catch up, it walked slowly purposely. But when Ahe came up and wanted to catch it, it suddenly leaped a long distance away from him, which made Ahe very angry.

When the deer lured Ahe to the South China Sea, Ahe gritted his teeth, pulled out an arrow and shot at the deer, but the arrow flew up into the sky. He drew a second arrow, but the arrow flew down into the sea. He drew eight arrows in a row, but all were lost. He pulled out the last arrow, slowly approached the deer, prepared the arrow and drew the bow. Just as he was about to let the arrow go, the deer suddenly let out a long cry. Turning around, the deer slowly walked towards Ahe and turned into a beautiful girl. Ahe was stunned with surprise and joy. The girl came shyly with smile, put her right hand on Ahe's shoulder, and sang gently,

"My dear is strong and handsome,

I'd like to give my heart to him.

My dear is courageous,

And hardworking all the time."

Ahe asked embarrassedly,

"Where are you from?

Like a flower in blossom,

Such a beautiful lady,

Where can I find?"

The deer girl blushed, lowered her head and replied,

"Goddess of Wuzhishan Mountain,

My nickname is Ajiao.

If my dear wants water,

I would like to be a ladle."

Hearing these words, Ahe was like drinking three bowls of Shanlan rice wine. He put his arms around the deer girl's waist and sang,

"Your song is so sweet,

Even sweeter than the nightingale.

Today I got a treasure,

And Kapok blossoms in full."

The deer girl blushed even more like a drunken betel nut. She buried her head in Ahe's arms and whispered,

"My dear will not be alone,

My dear won't be lonely any more.

I will make bed for you at night,

And wait at home in the daytime."

Ahe was deeply touched and couldn't help holding the deer girl in his arms.

Soon Ahe and the deer girl got married. Later they gave birth to two sons and two daughters. Then the sons and daughters got married and had their own children. Their descendants all lived there and the village became a big one. Later, people called the village Luhuitou (Deer-turning-around) Village.

## 故事十六  落笔洞

在海南岛天涯海角附近，有个山洞，名叫落笔洞。洞里有个宽阔的大厅，一张石桌摆在中央，桌前的石椅上坐着一位目光炯炯、英姿勃勃的少年武将。石桌上放着一个大石砚，三支石笔从山洞的顶端并排垂下，直指石砚；三股泉水沿着笔杆缓缓滴进石砚。在武将周围还有许多神态奇特的石像：有骑马挥剑的，有手持弓箭的。这些石像是怎么来的呢？

传说有一天，有一位名叫董亲的老人，带着独生女儿董梅出海捕鱼。船到远海，不料碰上了几只官家的船。官船横冲直撞，董亲父女竭力回避，但还是来不及躲开，最终被撞得粉碎。董亲一下子就被海涛吞没了。董梅侥幸抓到一块船板，游了三天三夜。到第四天，她再也游不动了。这时，她忽然看见空中亮起一道红光，接着，一位英俊的小伙子从天上轻轻飘了下来。他把董梅救上岸，还送她回家。董梅回家之后，用最好的酒菜招待他，因为天色已晚，便挽留他在家中过夜。第二天，等董梅醒来，那小伙子早已不知去向了。

不久，董梅怀孕了。奇怪的是，她怀孕三年才生下一个男孩。她给孩子取了个名字叫董公殿。董梅把孩子视为掌上明珠，可是董公殿到了九岁还不会讲话。董公殿十周岁那天，母亲带他上街市，跑了半天，来到鱼市上，董公殿看见一条大鲤鱼，突然开口说："阿妈，我要那条大鲤鱼。"董梅听到孩子第一次开口说话，心中很是高兴，便把那条鲤鱼买了回来。回家后，董公殿剖开鱼腹一看，发现里面有三支箭、一把弓、一把宝剑、三支笔和一个墨砚。那宝剑上还刻有"崖州董公殿"几个字。董公殿欢喜若狂，董梅却又喜又惊。

原来那时候皇帝欺压黎民，常常来崖州抢掠财宝和妇女，人们都恨死他了，董公殿想设计杀死皇帝。当天晚上睡觉前，董公殿对母亲说："阿妈，记住明早四时叫我起床。"董梅问他为什么，他不肯讲。董梅只好听从儿子的吩咐，在房里点灯没有睡觉，等待时辰的到来。母亲劝他好好睡觉，时间一到就叫醒他，但董公殿不放心，总是问个不停。母亲听到鸡叫头一遍，便说："孩子，时间到了。"董公殿一骨碌爬起床来，急忙取出宝箭，用力向北射去。只听见"嗖"的一声，宝箭闪着绿光，直往皇帝的宫殿飞去。

说来也巧，这时皇帝正准备上朝，手扶龙椅刚想坐下。忽然一声巨响，震得宫殿东摇西晃。随着一道绿光飞来，他把头一歪，"嚓"的一声，一支利箭穿过皇冠插在龙椅的靠背上，吓得皇帝魂飞魄散，连忙五体投地拜天求饶。他命左右卫士上前来拔箭，可是拔了半天，那箭像生了根似的，任凭你九牛二虎之力，还是拔不动。皇帝急忙上前，发现箭上刻有"崖州董公殿"五个字，连忙发号施令："快，快出兵崖州，抓住董公殿！"

董公殿发箭后，便将家中的谷子、粟子和玉米各量一斗，分别用三个水缸把它们浸起来，严严密密地封盖好，然后分别写上"三个月成士兵""三个月成马""三个月成兵器"的字样。

可是，不到三个月，皇帝派来的官兵已渡过了琼州海峡，登上了海岛。董公殿看见旗号，知道皇帝没有死，又看见寨外旌旗林立，战马嘶鸣，连忙把浸在缸里的谷子、粟子、玉米全倒在地上，叫了一声"变"。顷刻之间，这些东西变成了数不清的头包红巾、身着蓝衣绿裤的士兵。这些士兵个个骑着战马，手拿刀戟剑戈，威风凛凛。董公殿骑着战马大呼一声"冲"，那些士兵便跟董公殿一起杀了过去。官兵一见来了这么多兵马，吓得屁滚尿流，转身就逃。

皇帝又派武将黑蛇精领数万兵马，前来攻打崖州。董公殿与他们打了整整三日三夜，才把官兵打退。

董公殿打赢之后，寨里男男女女载歌载舞，捧出山兰酒慰劳董公殿。正当大家饮酒欢乐的时候，官兵射来一支暗箭。董梅眼明手快，一个箭步冲上去将董公殿推开，箭就不偏不倚地射中董梅的胸膛，她当场身亡。董公殿伏在母亲身上放声大哭，乡亲们个个愤怒不已，发誓要向官兵讨还血债。董公殿与乡亲们把董梅的尸体埋在海边沙滩上，不料刚埋好，官兵又厮杀过来。董公殿急忙抵抗，但因为官兵众多，他的兵马又是不足三个月幻化出来的，羽毛未丰，力量不足，只好沿着海滨边打边退。他忽然发现前面有一块巨石，堵住了他们的去路，他们进退两难。董公殿取下弓箭，把第三支宝箭对准巨石射去，只听得"轰隆"一声巨响，山摇地动，那块巨石裂开了一个大洞。董公殿和部下急忙进了石洞，抗击官兵。他们从洞内掷出无数石头，一块巨石把黑蛇精的头颅砸破，黑蛇精当场死亡。剩下的官兵见领头的已死，只得抱头鼠窜。

可是，董公殿他们进了那个石洞，也出不来了。日长年久，他们变为石像。因为这个山洞顶上还吊着三支石笔，人们就叫它为落笔洞。埋葬董梅的海滩上，长出了一根高高的大石柱，这就是今天的"南天一柱"。

## Luobidong[①]

Near the south end of Hainan Island, there is a cave named Luobidong. In the cave there is a wide hall, and a stone table is in the center of the hall. A bright-eyed vigorous young military general is sitting on the stone chair in front of the table. On the stone table stands a large ink stone, three stone pens align side by side from the top of the cave, pointing directly at the ink stone, and three springs drip along the pen holders slowly into the ink stone. Around the stone general are many stone statues with peculiar looks, some waving swords on horse backs,

---

① Hanging Pen Cave.

some holding bows and arrows. How did these stone statues come into being?

According to legend, one day an old man named Dong Qin went fishing with his only daughter Dong Mei. When their boat sailed a long distance to the open sea, it unexpectedly met with several official ships. The official ships sailed recklessly so Dong Qin and his daughter tried to avoid those ships but failed. Finally their boat was smashed into pieces. Dong Qin was swallowed up by sea waves at once. Dong Mei caught a board by chance and swam in the sea for three days and nights. On the fourth day, she could not swim any more. Suddenly she saw a red light appearing in the sky, and then a handsome young man flew down from the sky. He rescued Dong Mei and sent her home. When Dong Mei came home, she served him the best dishes and drinks. As it was too late, he was asked to stay overnight. The next day, when Dong Mei woke up, the young man had gone.

Before long, Dong Mei became pregnant. Strangely enough, she didn't give birth to a baby boy until three years later. She named the baby Dong Gongdian. Dong Mei regarded her son as the apple of her eye, but Dong Gongdian couldn't speak a word until he was nine years old. On the day when Dong Gongdian was ten years old, his mother took him to the market. They strolled there for a long while till they came to the fish stall. When Dong Gongdian saw a big carp, he suddenly opened his mouth and said, "Mom, I want that big carp." This was the first time that Dong Mei heard her son speak, so she was very happy and bought the carp back. After returning home, Dong Gongdian cut the fish's belly open and found three arrows, a bow, a sword, three pens and an ink stone in it. The sword was inscribed with the words "Yazhou Dong Gongdian". Dong Gongdian was wild with joy, but Dong Mei was both happy and surprised.

At that time, the emperor oppressed the people and often sent his men to rob treasures and women in Yazhou, so people hated him very much. Dong Gongdian planned to kill the emperor. Before going to bed that night, Dong Gongdian said to his mother, "Mom, remember to wake me up at 4 o'clock tomorrow morning." Dong Mei asked him why but he refused to explain. Dong Mei had to follow her son's order, lighting a lamp in the room and waiting for the time to come. She persuaded her son to go to sleep and promised she would wake him up as soon as the time came, but Dong Gongdian was not at ease and kept asking if the time had come. When Dong Mei heard the cock crow for the first time, she said, "It's time, son." Dong Gongdian got up all at once, took out one arrow and shot northward. Whoosh! With a green light flashing, the arrow flew straight to the emperor's palace.

Coincidentally, the emperor was attending the early morning imperial court session, and was about to sit down on the armchair. Suddenly a loud sound shook the palace, and with the sound flied in a green light. The emperor cocked his head, and a sharp arrow pierced through the crown into the back of the armchair. The emperor was so frightened that he knelt down to pray the heaven for mercy. Then he ordered the guards to pull out the arrow, but the arrow seemed to have taken root. No matter how great strength they used, they could not pull it out. The emperor moved forward and found the arrow engraved with the words "Yazhou Dong Gongdian", so he immediately issued an order, "Quick, go to Yazhou, seize Dong Gongdian!"

After the arrow was shot, Dong Gongdian took a bucket of foxtail millet, a bucket of millet and a bucket of corn, soaked them in three water vats, sealed them tightly, and wrote the sentences "Change into soldiers after three months.", "Change into horses after three months." and "Change into weapons after three months." on each vat respectively.

However, in less than three months, the emperor's troops crossed the Qiongzhou Strait and boarded the island. When Dong Gongdian saw the banner, he knew that the emperor was not dead. Soon flags reached outside the village, and horses' neighs could be heard. Dong Gongdian quickly poured out all the foxtail millet, millet and corn from the vats on the floor and chanted "Change!". In an instant, these things turned into countless soldiers in red scarves and blue and green uniforms. Those soldiers were all riding horses and holding swords. Dong Gongdian shouted "Rush!" on his horse, and all the soldiers rushed after him. As soon as the official troops saw so many soldiers and horses coming, they were frightened and fled back.

Then the emperor sent the Black Snake Demon general to attack Yazhou with tens of thousands of soldiers and horses. Dong Gongdian fought against them for three days and nights and repulsed them.

After Dong Gongdian won the battle, men and women in the village sang and danced, holding Shanlan rice wine to salute Dong Gongdian. Just when everyone was drinking and enjoying themselves, an arrow was shot from a hiding place by the official soldiers. Dong Mei had a sharp eye and saw clearly. She rushed up quickly and pushed Dong Gongdian away. The arrow directly hit Dong Mei in the chest and she died immediately. Dong Gongdian leant over his mother's body and cried bitterly. The villagers were furious and vowed that blood will have blood. No sooner had Dong Gongdian and his fellow villagers buried Dong Mei's body in the beach than the troops fought back again. Dong Gongdian fought back in a hurry, but the enemy troop was so large in number, while his horses and soldiers were cultivated in less than three months and were not strong enough, so they had to retreat along the coast. Suddenly they found a huge stone in front of them, blocking their way. They were in a dilemma. Dong Gongdian took down the bow and shot the last arrow at the boulder. With a loud bang, the mountain began to shake and the boulder cracked and formed a big hole. Dong Gongdian and his followers rushed into the cave to fight against the officers and soldiers. They threw out countless stones from the cave. A huge stone smashed the head of the Black Snake Demon and it died instantly. The remaining soldiers saw that their leader was dead so they all fled away immediately.

However, after Dong Gongdian and his men entered the cave, they couldn't come out. As time went by, they turned into stone statues. Since there were three stone pens hanging from the top of the cave, people called it Luobidong. On the beach where Dong Mei was buried, a tall stone pillar grew up and this is today's Nantianyizhu (also known as the Pillar of the Southern Heaven).

## 故事十七　亚龙湾

三亚市西南部有个叫野猪山的岛。

相传很久很久以前，岛上有很多野猪，附近黎胞在两位年轻族长的带领下，常到岛上猎野猪。两位族长武艺高强，善寻踪迹，每次打野猪都满载而归。可是，有一年中秋的夜晚，两位年轻族长突然失踪，留下的只是两摊鲜血和巨大的野猪蹄印。众人都认为是野猪王干的。两位武艺高强的族长都已经被害，还有谁能击败野猪王呢？众人把目光投向青年猎手亚龙身上。亚龙苦练三年武艺，然后向小岛进发，去杀野猪王。

野猪王被惊动，出来迎战。双方展开一场激战，从岛南杀到岛北，从岛东杀到岛西，直杀得天昏地暗。虽然亚龙武艺高强，却始终不能打败野猪王。

野猪王越来越疯狂，下村毁坏农作物、捕捉牲畜，还咬小孩子，黎民不得安居。亚龙想：野猪王太厉害，只能与它斗智。亚龙听说见血封喉树的树汁最毒，他用力砍破见血封喉树的树皮，取其汁涂在弓箭头上，然后上山斗野猪王。野猪王猛冲过来时，亚龙眼明手快，一箭射中野猪王的头部，野猪王倒地死去了。可惜亚龙因手有伤口，也被见血封喉毒汁染上，不久也死了。亚龙为民除害而献身，人们把他埋在岭下的海滩上，从此这里就被称为亚龙湾。

## Yalong Bay

There is a small island named Boar Hill in the southwest part of Sanya.

According to legend, a long time ago, there were many boars on the island. Under the leadership of two young patriarchs of the Li nationality, the neighboring Li people often went to the island to hunt boars. The two patriarchs were highly skilled in hunting, so every time they went hunting boars, they could come back with fruitful prey. However, on the night of the Mid-Autumn Festival one year, the two young patriarchs suddenly disappeared, only left two pools of blood and some huge hoof prints of boar. Everyone thought it was done by the Boar King. Now that the two patriarchs had been killed, who else could defeat the Boar King? Everyone expected the young hunter Yalong to take revenge, so Yalong practiced martial arts and hunting skills for three years, and then set out to the island to fight against the Boar King.

The Boar King was startled and came out to fight against Yalong. A fierce battle was launched between them and they fought from the south to the north, from the east to the west of the island. Although Yalong was highly skilled in Kungfu, he could hardly defeat the Boar King.

The Boar King was getting more and more crazy. It came to the village to destroy crops and kill livestock, and even bite children. The Li people could not live in peace anymore. Yalong thought that the Boar King was so powerful that he could only win it through wisdom. Yalong heard that the sap of upas-tree was the most poisonous liquid, so he slashed the bark of the upas-tree, smeared the sap onto the arrowheads, and climbed up the mountain to fight against the Boar King. As soon as the Boar King came hurtling towards him, Yalong aimed at the Boar King and shot it to death in head only by one arrow. Unfortunately, due to Yalong's wounds in his hand, the poisonous sap infected the wound and caused his death soon after. As Yalong dedicated himself to killing the Boar King for the Li people, they buried him in the beach under the mountain. Thereafter the place was called Yalong Bay.

## 故事十八　万泉河

万泉河发源于五指山区。

"万泉河水清又清",人们一直这么传诵着。据说,那清流是天宫七仙女的功劳。

古时候,那里没有河流,居住在这一带的人们艰难度日。有一年,不知从哪里来了一伙风魔,刮起十二级台风,把房屋刮得砖倒瓦飞,农作物被刮得颗粒无收。随后又来了一伙火魔,烧得赤地千里,人们无法耕种,只好离乡背井逃荒而去。人们呼天唤地,万道眼泪流成了一条河,后人称为万泉河。但河水是混浊的,带有咸味。

天宫的七仙女不甘寂寞,相约到凡间游玩,看到这里有条河,便脱下仙衣,跳进河水沐浴。七仙女在天上修炼得肌肤雪白,所以把混浊的河水也变澄清了。七仙女虽然回天宫去了,但却给人间留下了清流。自此,万物复苏,离乡背井的人们重返家园,造房建屋,勤耕忙种,万泉河畔出现了万木苍翠、鸟语花香、人旺业兴的美景。

## **Wanquan River**[①]

The Wanquan River originated from the Wuzhishan Mountain.

"Water of the Wanquan River is crystal clear", people have been singing in this way. Do you know why? It is said that the crystal clear water owed to the seven fairies from the heavenly palace.

---

① Ten-thousand-people's Tears River.

In ancient times, there was no river in this area and people lived a hard life. One year, a gang of wind demons coming from nowhere caused a twelve-level typhoon, which blew off the bricks and tiles of the houses and destroyed the crops and left nothing for people to live on. Then, a gang of fire demons came and set fire to the field, causing the barren land to be unsuitable for farming. People had no choice but left their hometown to flee from famine. They cried to the heaven and the earth, and their tears formed a river which was later called the Wanquan River. But the water of the river used to be muddy and salty.

The seven fairies from the heavenly palace could not bear the loneliness in heaven, so they came together to visit the mortal world. When they saw the river, they took off their clothes and bathed in it. As the seven fairies had cultivated themselves in the heavenly palace for a long time, their skins were as white as snow so that the muddy water was purified and became crystal clear. Although the seven fairies had gone back to the heavenly palace, they left the crystal clear river to the mortal world. Then things there began to come back to life. People who had fled away began to come back and rebuilt their houses, plowed their fields and grew crops. Thereafter, on both sides of the Wanquan River appeared beautiful scenery with trees flourishing, birds singing, flowers blooming, and people enjoying prosperous lives.

# 故事十九　天涯湾与南天一柱

传说很久很久以前，有一条庞大的蓝色的龙从北方飞临南天，偷吃了南天天宫里的一颗宝石，被守卫宝石的分管姓氏的僧人发现了。他立即拿起一根"分氏棍"指向这条蓝色的龙的脖子，一股巨大的魔力使这颗宝石死死地卡在它的喉咙里，它吞不下、吐不出，卡在嘴里含着。

这位分管姓氏的僧人早已在南天把人类的姓氏划分好了，准备起程飞往西天，但还没有物色到一个可靠的僧徒来接替他守卫宝石，现在看到这条蓝色的龙含住宝石，他有了主意。他用"分氏棍"朝天空划了个圆圈，顿时，天空上闪出了一个耀眼的光环，从蓝天上旋转落下，翻腾的蓝龙被镇在地面。不久，这条蓝龙变成广阔碧蓝的天涯湾，那颗含在嘴里的金宝石变成了南天一柱。

## Tianya Bay and Nantianyizhu

According to legend, a long time ago, a giant blue dragon flew from the north to the Southern Heaven. It stole a gem from the heavenly palace of the Southern Heaven and swallowed it. This was immediately found by the guarding monk who was responsible for distributing human surnames. The immortal monk pointed a surname distributing stick at the neck of the blue dragon, and the powerful magic made the gem stuck in the throat of the blue dragon who was unable to swallow it or spit it out.

It happened that the immortal monk in the Southern Heaven had distributed all the mortals' surnames and was ready to fly back to the Western Heaven, but he couldn't find a reliable disciple to take over the gem-guard task from him. Seeing the blue dragon with the gem in its throat, he came up with an idea. The monk drew a circle towards the sky by using the surname distributing stick. At once, a dazzling aureole appeared in the sky, fell down and revolved around the blue dragon, which trapped the blue dragon on the ground. Before long, the blue dragon turned into the vast blue water later called Tianya Bay, and the golden gem in its mouth turned into the Nantianyizhu, the Pillar of the Southern Heaven.

# 故事二十　甘工鸟

很久很久以前，在海南岛美丽的七仙岭脚下，有一个漂亮的黎族女孩叫阿甘，她唱的山歌能迷住天上的飞鸟，她跳的舞能让彩云围着转，她织的黎锦能引蝴蝶飞来。邻寨有一个英俊的青年猎手叫劳海，他勤劳勇敢，箭法百发百中，能一箭射中天上的飞鸟、地上奔跑的野兽。在日常生活劳动中，阿甘和劳海产生了爱情。这天生的一对璧人常在七仙岭温泉湖边倾吐衷肠，在椰树下许下山盟海誓。

这事传到了大霸峒主那里去了，他的儿子心狠手辣，长一身毒疮，又丑又臭，他得知阿甘生得标致，早已垂涎三尺，做梦都想夺过来做媳妇。有一天，大霸峒主真的派媒婆送槟榔和聘礼上门来定亲，并限三天后派人来迎亲。可是金银财宝也动摇不了阿甘和她爹娘的心，阿甘把聘礼退了回去，死也不嫁给黑心郎。阿甘很伤心，当夜下山把内情告诉劳海。三天后，大霸峒主果然派一帮人马来抢亲。劳海为了不让心上人落入虎穴，奋勇抵抗，用弓箭射倒了几个家奴。在搏斗中，劳海被砍伤昏倒在地，家奴趁机把阿甘劫走了。阿甘被关在旧谷仓里严加防守。一天，一只燕子从窗外飞过，阿甘祈求燕子捎个信给劳海让他来救她。燕子告诉她逃走的方法，教她把身上戴的银环银链舂成一对羽翅插在身上就可以飞出去了。阿甘一一照着燕子的嘱咐去做，终于飞了出去。大霸峒主得知到手的儿媳飞走了，拼命地叫家奴追回来。阿甘为反抗强迫婚姻，远走高飞，誓不回头。劳海也立志愿为爱情化作一只鸟，飞上七仙岭寻找心爱的阿甘。

从此，乡亲们再也见不到阿甘和劳海了，只是在天空中经常见到一对鸟儿逍遥自在地飞翔、歌唱，"甘工""甘工"鸣叫不断，人们都称这种鸟为甘工鸟。

# Gangong Bird

Long long ago, at the foot of the Qixianling Mountain of Hainan Island, there was a beautiful girl in the Li ethnic group named Agan. When Agan sang the folk songs, the flying birds were fascinated; when Agan danced, the colorful clouds danced around her; the brocades she wove were so vivid that they could attract butterflies. Meanwhile there was a handsome young hunter in the neighboring village named Laohai who was industrious and courageous. Laohai was highly skilled in archery. He could shoot the flying birds in the sky or the running wild beast on the ground with one shot. As time went by, Agan and Laohai fell in love with each other. This perfect couple used to express true love to each other by the spring lake in the Qixianling Mountain and take the pledge of eternal love under the coconut trees.

Agan's beauty was heard by the head of the village and his son. The son who was fierce-hearted, ugly and smelly with poisonous sores had drooled over Agan for a long time and even dreamed of taking her as his wife. So one day, the head of the village sent a matchmaker to Agan's home with areca-nuts and presents to make Agan get engaged to his son. The matchmaker left word that Agan would be escorted to the wedding three days later. Money and treasure did not change the minds of Agan and her parents. Agan rejected the betrothal presents and said that she would rather die than marry a man with evil mind. Agan was so sad that she went downhill that night and told Laohai what had happened. Three days later, the head of the village sent a gang of family servants to snatch Agan. Laohai fought against the gang bravely to protect his lover. He shot down several servants with his bow and arrows, but was also slashed and fainted on the ground, then the servants seized the chance to snatch Agan away. Agan was locked in an old barn and guarded strictly. One day, when a swallow was flying past the window, Agan begged it to take a message to Laohai so that Laohai would come to save her. The swallow taught her how to make her silver rings and chains into a pair of wings, and use the wings to fly away. Agan did what the swallow taught her and really flew away. As soon as the head of the village heard that his daughter-in-law had flew away, he desperately ordered his servants to catch her back. In order to resist this forced marriage, Agan flew away and swore never to return home. Laohai, in order to follow his lover, also turned into a bird and flew to the Qixianling Mountain to look for Agan.

Since then, the villagers had never seen Agan and Laohai again, but they could often see a pair of birds flying freely in the sky and chirping with the sound of "gangong, gangong". Thus, people called such birds Gangong Birds.

## 故事二十一 椰子的由来

海南岛最早的先民是黎族。黎族人民经常遭到异邦侵略军的侵扰，有位英勇的黎族青年叫龙果，他率领黎族人民抗击侵略者。因侵略者兵多势众，龙果率领黎族人民撤退到五指山区的高山密林中安营扎寨。但队伍中出了叛徒，叛徒带领着侵略军偷袭黎寨，龙果在乡亲们的掩护下逃进深山，脱险了。敌人扑了空，就将寨中一年长老汉抓来严酷拷审，要他供出龙果的去向。老汉宁死不屈，敌人便砍下他的头，吊在旗杆上。突然旗杆越长越高，敌人忙拔箭乱射。旗杆变成高高的椰子树，老汉的头变成圆圆的椰果，箭变成了羽状的椰叶。龙果后来重整队伍，率领众黎民最终战胜了侵略者。为了纪念宁死不屈的黎族老汉，黎族人民精心护育种植椰树，使它遍布海南岛。

## The Origin of Coconut

The earliest ancestors of Hainan Island were the Li nationality. The Li people used to be invaded by foreign invaders. There was a brave Li youth named Longguo who led the Li people to fight against the invaders. Due to the overwhelming number of invaders, Longguo had to lead the Li people to retreat to the dense forest of the Wuzhishan Mountain to settle down. But there was a traitor in the team who led the invaders to attack the Li people. Longguo escaped deep into the mountains under the cover of the villagers. Seeing that they couldn't catch Longguo, the invaders caught an old man in the village and tortured him severely. They forced him to tell where Longguo was, but the old man would rather die than surrender. The invaders cut off his head and hung it on a flagpole. Suddenly, the flagpole began to grow higher and higher. The invaders were terrified and rushed to shoot arrows at the flagpole. But the flagpole turned into a tall coconut tree, the old man's head turned into a round coconut, and the arrows turned into feathery coconut leaves. Later Longguo reorganized his troops and finally defeated the invaders. In order to commemorate the indomitable old man, the Li people carefully planted and protected the coconut tree, making it spread all over Hainan Island.

## 故事二十二 黎族三月三节

"三月三"是黎家青年男女欢乐的节日。每年农历三月三日这一天,男女盛装打扮、跳舞、唱歌,欢庆这一传统佳节。

远古时候,洪水泛滥,淹没了平原和山岭,吞没了大地的一切,只剩下了天妃和观音兄妹两人。他们抱住了葫芦瓢,在滔天的洪水中到处漂泊。漂啊漂啊,他们漂流到昌化江畔的燕窝岭,被一棵大榕树的树丫卡住了。过了些时候,洪水慢慢消退了,兄妹俩总算活了下来,可是,大地上什么都没有了,只剩下他俩孤零零地生活着。兄妹俩决定分头去寻找亲人,临走前,两人约定三月三日回到燕窝岭相会。他们走遍了天涯海角,到处都见不到人迹。哥哥找不到女郎配偶,妹妹找不到男子成亲。年长月久,眼见兄妹俩快要衰老,人就要绝种了。妹妹暗地里拿定主意,在自己脸上刺上了花纹,这一来,哥哥便认不出纹脸的妹妹。于是,在一年的三月三日,兄妹俩就在燕窝岭下结为夫妻,生儿育女。婚后,他们朝出暮归,勤耕勤作,在昌化江畔挖水塘养鱼,在燕窝岭下种植木棉、杧果和"山棯子"①,还在半山腰开凿一个石洞居住。洞的上面是悬崖陡壁,野兽不敢来侵犯;洞的下面是峭壁万丈,山洪水涨也淹不到。每年三月三日,正是山花烂漫、"山棯子"飘香的时候,观音和天妃便率着子孙们一起载歌载舞,迎接春天的到来。

后来不知过了多久,天妃和观音死在山洞里,化成了观音石。黎家子孙后代为纪念天妃和观音,也就把石洞取名为娘母洞。每逢三月三日,男女老少都要携带用糯米做的糕点、粽子放在洞口祭拜。这一天,从白天到夜晚,热闹非凡。他们仿效祖先,在劳动中

---

① 即桃金娘。

寻找伴侣，夜里，燃起一堆堆篝火，用歌声表达爱情。从此，"三月三"也就成为男女青年定情的日子。

## The Double Third Festival of the Li Nationality

The third day of the third month in the lunar calendar is a joyous festival, known as the Double Third Festival, for the young men and women of the Li nationality. Every year on this day, men and women dress up, dance and sing to celebrate this traditional festival.

According to legend, in ancient times, floods inundated the plains and mountains, engulfing everything on the earth. A brother named Tianfei and a sister named Guanyin escaped death by grabbing a gourd and floating in the flood. They floated along the Changhuajiang River for a long time till they were blocked by a large banyan tree in the river near the Yanwoling Mountain. After a while, the flood water gradually receded, and the brother and the sister survived. However, there was nothing left on the earth, and only the two of them lived alone. They decided to part from each other to find their relatives. Before seperation, they promised to return to the Yanwoling Mountain on the third day of the third lunar month to meet each other. They traveled all over the world but could not find anyone else. The brother couldn't find a woman to be his wife, and the sister could not find a man to marry. As time passed by, the brother and the sister got older and older, and human was about to extinct. The sister secretly made up her mind. She tattooed on her face so that her brother could not recognize her. Therefore, on the third day of the third lunar month of one year, the brother and the sister got married in the Yanwoling Mountain and gave birth to children. They worked diligently from dawn to sunset everyday to make a living. They dug pools for fish-farming near the Changhuajiang River bank, and grew ceiba, mango and chinaberry trees in the Yanwoling Mountain. They also dug a stone cave on the hillside to live in. The upside of the cave was steep cliff, so the wild beast did not dare to invade; below the cave was also high cliff, so even the torrential flood could not reach the cave. Every year on the third day of the third lunar month, when the flowers in the mountain bloomed and the chinaberry trees began to release fragrance, Guanyin and Tianfei would lead their children and grandchildren to sing and dance together to welcome the arrival of spring.

Later, Tianfei and Guanyin died in the cave and turned into stones. In order to commemorate them, the descendants of the Li nationality named the cave Mother Cave. On every Double Third Festival, the Li people of all ages and both sexes will put the sticky rice cakes and dumplings at the entrance of the cave for worship and the atmosphere of the whole day and night is very lively. Following the tradition of their ancestors, the Li people will find their mates during work, light up piles of bonfire at night and express their love by singing songs. From then on, Double Third Festival also becomes a day for young men and women to express love.

# 故事二十三　纹面的传说

相传在很久很久以前，有一户贫苦人家生下了一个非常漂亮的小女孩，名字叫乌娜。乌娜不满九个月的时候，父亲便死去了，母女俩相依为命，过着孤苦的日子。乌娜很聪明，六岁就会绣花，八岁就会帮助母亲下田种地。乌娜唱的歌，天上的云彩也会停下来倾听，水上的鱼儿听了，也欢喜欢得待在水面上，不愿离去。村里的人个个都说乌娜是个好姑娘，姑娘们特别喜欢和乌娜在一起种地、唱歌和绣花。乌娜到了十三岁，长得如天仙一样美丽，不少年轻小伙子都来向她求婚，每天傍晚，乌娜的家门口都是热热闹闹的。可是乌娜早已看上了邻居的劳可哥哥。劳可的家也像乌娜家一样穷苦，家里有年老的父母，已经不能干活了，全靠劳可一人上山打柴和狩猎过着苦日子。十五岁的劳可已长得很威武、健壮，一肩能挑五百斤①，两拳能打死一只山豹。村里的人都说劳可是个勇敢、勤劳的好青年，和乌娜是天生的一对。

有一年，皇帝在民间挑选美女，看中了乌娜姑娘，并限定在七天之内，送她入宫里。乌娜和她的母亲痛哭流涕，不知道怎么办才好。劳可知道了，拿起弓箭要与皇帝拼命，寨里的人都为他们的不幸遭遇担忧。

五天过去了，进宫的期限快到了，老人们对乌娜的母亲说："由我们来做主，让乌娜和劳可结婚吧！"青年们说："我们不能让乌娜妹妹投入火海，你们快把婚事办了。"劳可的父母和乌娜的母亲也都同意，事情就这样决定了。不料第六天晚上，正当人们热热闹闹庆贺劳可与乌娜成亲的时候，皇帝连夜派了兵丁赶来抢亲。一

---

① 1斤=500克。

## 第五章
黎族经典民间故事汉英对照

看来的人马很多,难以抵挡,寨里的人都劝劳可和乌娜赶快逃走。就这样,劳可与乌娜离开了父母,离开了家乡,翻山越岭,连夜逃走。

第二天天亮,劳可和乌娜逃到了海边,只见前面的去路被大海阻住,后面的追兵正向他们赶来。乌娜紧紧地依偎着劳可,伤心地哭泣起来。劳可说:"妹啊!莫伤心,我们是活着成双对,死了不分离。"乌娜擦干了眼泪,两眼望着劳可,也说:"哥啊!我们至死也不分开。"正说着,后面的追兵赶上来了,劳可和乌娜手拉着手走到海边,决意双双跳下海去。正在危急的时候,忽然间,乌天黑地,狂风呼呼,海浪滚滚,海面上漂来一块大木头,劳可和乌娜赶忙跳下去,抓住木头,随着波浪漂流而去。皇帝的兵丁赶到后,只好眼巴巴地看着他们漂远。

劳可和乌娜在海上漂呀,漂呀,漂流了三天三夜,到了一个孤岛上,这个岛便是今天的海南岛。他们怕皇帝再来追赶,就到山上去居住。他们用草和树枝盖成像船一样的房子,表示他们是从别处漂流过来的。劳可和乌娜在山上安下了家,就靠着狩猎度日子。有一天,乌娜对劳可说:"如果有谷子、瓜子和各种种子就好了,我们可以在这里种地。"话刚说完,忽然有一只斑鸠飞来,停在树上叫着说:"咕咕咕!你说的我都有。"他们感到奇怪,劳可马上拿起弓箭,把斑鸠射了下来。果然不错,斑鸠肚里各种种子都有。于是,劳可和乌娜便在山上烧山种山兰稻了,他们的生活过得很好。

隔了一年,不幸的事情又发生了。乌娜的下落被皇帝打听到了,皇帝带了兵丁,亲自渡海来抢乌娜。兵丁把劳可和乌娜住的地方团团围住,劳可和乌娜拉起弓箭,与兵丁对抗,利箭射死了许多兵丁。可是兵丁越来越多,劳可被打伤了,忙叫乌娜快往深山里逃跑。乌娜越过了高山,爬过了峻岭,穿过了茂密的丛林,弄得一身衣服全被荆棘刺破了,手上、腿上和整个身体都布满了一道道伤痕。后来乌娜跑得精疲力竭,再也没有力气往前跑了。她心如刀割,伸手从树上拔下一根尖利的荆棘,往自己的脸上猛刺,刺得斑斑点点，血迹满面。后来乌娜还是被兵丁捉住了，但皇帝一看乌娜的脸面变成那副模样，连忙吼道："你们这些混蛋，这样的女人要她来做什么？"乌娜就被放掉了。

后来，劳可找到了乌娜，便一起到更荒凉的深山里去居住。他们还是种山兰稻、狩猎，日子过得很和美。不久，他们生育了子女，为了不再遭皇帝的迫害，乌娜要她的女儿也在脸上刺上一道道的疤痕。这样，妇女纹脸的风俗就一代代传了下来。

## The Legend about Facial Tattoo

Long time ago, there was a poor family who gave birth to a very beautiful baby girl named Wuna. When Wuna was about nine months old, her father passed away, leaving her mother and her depending on each other. They lived a lonely and hard life. Wuna was very clever. She could do embroidery at six. At eight, she could help her mother do farming. When Wuna was singing, the clouds in the sky would stop to listen and the fish would stay quiet in the water rather than swimming. Everyone in the village praised her as a good girl and all girls liked farming, singing and doing embroidery with Wuna very much. When Wuna was thirteen, she turned to be as beautiful as a fairy and many young men wanted to propose to her. As a result, the doorstep of Wuna's home was crowded with young men at dusk everyday. However, Wuna had already been in love with her neighbor, Laoke. Laoke's family was as poor as Wuna's, and his parents were too old to work. So every day Laoke went into mountains to cut firewood and hunt to make a living. They led a very hard life. The fifteen-year-old Laoke was very strong. He could shoulder 250 kilograms' burden with one shoulder and punch a leopard to death with two fists. The villagers all said that Laoke was brave and diligent and could make a perfect couple with Wuna.

One year, the emperor looked for beauties in folk and Wuna was chosen. The emperor ordered to have Wuna sent to his palace within seven days. Wuna and her mother burst into tears and didn't know what to do. When Laoke knew about this, he took his bow and arrows and wanted to fight with the emperor. The villagers were worried about their fates.

Five days later, when the deadline of entering the palace was coming, the elder villagers said to Wuna's mother, "We should let Wuna and Laoke get married." All the young men said, "We won't allow Wuna to get into such a terrible situation. You should hold your wedding as soon as possible." Both Laoke's parents and Wuna's mother agreed with their marriage. Unexpectedly, on the sixth night, when the villagers were happily celebrating the wedding of Laoke and Wuna, the emperor sent soldiers to catch Wuna. Seeing that the coming soldiers were too many to resist, the villagers persuaded Laoke and Wuna to run away immediately. With no other choice, Laoke and Wuna had to leave their parents and hometown. They climbed over mountains overnight to escape from the soldiers.

At dawn the next day, Laoke and Wuna fled to a beach, but were blocked by the sea in front of them. Seeing that the soldiers were chasing right behind them, Wuna leaned close to Laoke and began to cry sadly. Laoke said, "My dear love, don't be sad. We will live in pair or die together." Wuna wiped away her tears, looked at Laoke and said, "My dear love, even death cannot separate us." At these words, the soldiers nearly caught up with them. Laoke and Wuna walked to the cliff hand in hand and decided to jump into the sea. At the critical time, the sky suddenly turned dark, the wind began to blow violently, the waves roared, and a large piece of wood was drifting on the sea. So Laoke and Wuna jumped into the sea, grabbed the wood and floated away with the wave. When the soldiers arrived, they could do nothing but watching them floating away.

  Laoke and Wuna floated on the sea for three days and nights and finally reached an isolated island which was today's Hainan Island. They were afraid that the emperor would catch up with them, so they settled in a mountain. They used grass and tree branches to build a boat-like hut, representing that they came from the other place. Laoke and Wuna settled down on the mountainside and made their living by hunting. One day, Wuna said to Laoke, "If only we had some grains, melon seeds and other kinds of seeds! Then, we can plant them for food here." As the words just fell from her lips, a turtledove flew over here, standing on the tree branch and chirped, "Coo, coo! I have everything you said." They felt surprised. Laoke took his bow and arrow to shoot down the turtledove. Just as what the turtledove said, there were various seeds in its belly. Therefore, Laoke and Wuna began to burn the mountains to plant Shanlan rice and other crops. Since then they had lived a very good life.

  One year later, misfortune happened again. The emperor found out Wuna's whereabouts, and he ordered the soldiers to sail across the sea to catch Wuna. The soldiers surrounded the place where Laoke and Wuna lived. Laoke and Wuna drew the bows and shot arrows to fight against the soldiers. With the sounds of "whoosh-whoosh" from the arrows, he shot many soldiers, but more and more soldiers were coming near. Laoke got wounded. He told Wuna to escape deep into the mountain area. Wuna climbed over the high and steep mountains, and ran through the dense jungle. Her clothes were all torn by thistles and thorns; her hands, legs and the whole body were all covered with wounds. Later, Wuna was exhausted and couldn't move anymore. She was heartbroken and plucked off a sharp throne from the tree and stabbed her own face with it fiercely.

Soon her face became besmeared with blood. Wuna was finally caught by the soldiers and sent to the emperor. However, when the emperor saw Wuna's disfigured face, he yelled hurriedly, "You bastards, how could you catch such an ugly woman for me?" Then Wuna was released.

Later, Laoke found Wuna. They went to a more desolate mountain area to live. They still planted Shanlan rice and hunted wild animals. They lived a peaceful and happy life, and had their own children. In order not to be harmed by the emperor any more, Wuna let her daughters make scars on their faces. Just like this, the custom of facial tattoo was passed down from generation to generation.

## 故事二十四　鼻箫

很久以前,一对黎族青年相爱了。临结婚前,这位姑娘到槟榔园采槟榔,被峒主发现了。当晚,姑娘被峒主抓去。峒主软硬兼施,要姑娘嫁给他。姑娘不同意,被关了起来。小伙子得知后焦急万分,他找了三天三夜,终于发现姑娘被关在密林中的一个小山洞里。两人无法相见,小伙子只好唱歌传情。峒主察知,又把小伙子抓了起来,割掉他的舌头,把他发配到一个荒远的山林里。过了一个多月,小伙子又在山洞边出现,他砍了一节白竹,并用鼻吹出自己的痛苦和思恋之情。姑娘心领意会,感泣不已。后来,小伙子被峒主抓去处死,死前托人将鼻箫转交给姑娘。姑娘接过鼻箫,悲痛欲绝。不久,姑娘在看守的帮助下逃出虎口,跪在小伙子坟前,把小伙子生前吹奏过的鼻箫曲吹奏了一遍又一遍。然后,姑娘怀揣鼻箫,安息在小伙子的墓前。从此,鼻箫便被一代又一代地传了下来。

## Nasal Flute

Long ago, a young couple of the Li nationality fell in love with each other. One day before their wedding, the girl went to the betel palm garden to pluck betel nuts, and was discovered by the head of the village. That night, the head of the village had the girl caught and forced her to marry him by using every possible means. The girl disagreed and was locked up. The young man was very anxious about the news. He searched for three days and nights and finally found that the girl was locked up in a small cave in the dense forest. They couldn't meet each other, so the young man had to sing songs to express his love. When the head of the village knew about this, he also had the young man caught, cut off his tongue, and banished him to a remote mountain forest. However, a month later the young man went back to the cave again. He cut a section of white bamboo and blew out his feelings of pain and love through his nostrils. The girl heard the music and was touched to weep. Later, the young man was caught and executed by the head of the village. Before death, the man had the nasal flute handed over to the girl by others. Seeing the nasal flute, the girl was very sad. Soon, with the help of the guard, the girl escaped from the cave. She knelt down in front of the young man's grave, playing the nasal flute over and over again. In the end the girl died in front of the young man's grave with the nasal flute in her arms. Since then, nasal flutes have been handed down from generation to generation.

# 故事二十五  黎族蜡染的来历

黎族蜡染工艺传说是由一位叫拜娜的黎族姑娘创造的。

拜娜是一位长得非常漂亮的黎族姑娘。拜娜不仅人长得好，歌也唱得很好，她一开口唱歌，不仅树上的鸟儿全部停下歌唱，连山中的百兽也被她的歌声迷住而一动不动。拜娜又是一个心灵手巧的姑娘，她可以把世上一切美好的东西都绣在她的筒裙上，而且活灵活现得让人以为是真的。一天，拜娜到山上去砍柴，看到一种树叶非常好看，深深地被迷住了，连树上的百灵鸟邀请她对歌，她都听不见。一会儿，她缓过神来，急忙把这种树叶采集下来，一片一片地贴在她的筒裙上。片刻，那树叶流出来的汁液在拜娜的筒裙上染出朵朵蓝色的花纹，拜娜一下子变得像一只孔雀鸟一样，美得连山泉都停止了流动。

于是，拜娜把这种叫作大青叶的多汁树叶摘回来制成染料，并用白蜡点衣施染，使衣服的色彩更加鲜艳亮丽。山寨里的人们看到拜娜穿着一身他们从来都没有见过的漂亮筒裙，纷纷上门拜师，拜娜便把这蜡染手艺毫不保留地传给寨里的人们。从此，蜡染手艺被黎族掌握并传承发展，代代流传至今。

## The Origin of Batik Technique of the Li Nationality

According to legend, the batik technique of the Li nationality was created by a Li girl named Baina.

Baina was very beautiful and could sing very well. Every time Baina started singing, the birds in trees would stop singing and the animals in mountains would stand still to listen carefully. Baina was also a ingenious girl. She could embroider all the beautiful things in the world on her skirt. Those embroideries were so lively and vivid that people mistook them as real things. One day, when Baina went to a mountain to cut firewood, she saw a kind of beautiful leaf. Baina was so fascinated with it that she even couldn't hear the lark on the tree inviting her to sing. After a while she collected herself and hurried to collect the leaves and paste them one by one on her skirt. For a moment, the sap from the leaves dyed Baina's skirt blue, which made Baina look like a peacock. She was so beautiful that even the spring stopped flowing.

So, Baina picked the juicy green leaves back to make dyes. With white wax, she dyed clothes with brighter colors. When the villagers saw Baina wearing a beautiful dress they had never seen before, they began to visit Baina and wanted to learn the techniques from her. Baina handed down the batik skills to the villagers without reservation. Since then, the batik technique has been handed down and developed by the Li people from generation to generation.

## 故事二十六　黎族倒挂树枝、撒灶灰的习俗

　　黎族都有这种习俗：凡是家里有病人，或者家人意外死亡的人家，都在檐上门前倒挂树枝，围绕屋子一周撒灶灰，其意在于赶鬼辟邪。

　　据说，从前有一个人，每天带着弓箭穿山越岭打猎过活。一天，在深山里的一棵大树下，猎人看见一位年轻姑娘坐在树墩上织布。姑娘太漂亮了，他竟然看呆了。不知站了多久，忽然，姑娘偏过头来对他微微一笑，他仿佛从梦中醒来，壮着胆子走近她的身旁搭话攀谈。一回生，二回熟，不久，他们相爱了，猎人把姑娘接回家里一起生活。

　　几个月过去了，这对夫妻倒也男欢女悦，相亲相爱。可就是猎人总感到心惊肉跳，他脸色焦黄，手不能拉开强弓，脚不能跳跃山涧。可怜一个壮实的小伙子却一天天消瘦下去。

　　一天，猎人在狩猎归途中遇上一个白发老人。老人对他端详一阵，说道："你的老婆是鬼，不是人啊！"猎人大吃一惊，但转而一想，含笑摇头，说啥也不相信。"不信？我教你。"老人把嘴伏在他的耳边上如此这般地述说了一阵，然后郑重地嘱咐："千万不能让她察觉，依我的法子去做，可救你一命。"说完便扬长而去。

　　猎人满腹狐疑、惴惴不安地回到家里。只见妻子笑脸相迎，仔细观察并无异样。当晚上床安歇，猎人翻来覆去，心事重重，说什么也不敢相信睡在身边美若山花的妻子竟然不是人。"鸡啼第一声，你就见分晓……"老人的话老是在耳边回响着。这一夜长极了，迷糊中，村寨里的雄鸡第一声晨啼传来，他赶快睁眼一瞧，"啊！"吓得他差点大声嚷叫。透过月光，他看到在他身边的竟然是一具白森森的骷髅。待他定神一看，奇怪，明明又是他那熟悉的妻子在安详

地沉睡着。经这一吓,他再也不能入眠。不久,妻子像往常一样,天不亮就下床煮早饭。这时他又想起老人跟他说的话:你老婆吃饭是假,用饭气熏蒸是真……于是,他便蹑手蹑脚地靠近厨房,眼睛对准裂开的泥墙缝。天啊!老人所描述的事儿果然就发生在眼前:昏暗的灶火,蒙蒙的蒸气,妻子双足钩住大梁,倒挂着身子,乌黑的长发垂遮着的脸庞差不多浸在煮开稀饭的锅里,更显得阴森可怕。他再也不敢多看一眼,暗下决心,不再迟疑,依着老人所教的法子去做。他悄悄地把瓦罐的底部凿破几个小洞,然后拿着山刀往后山奔去。天亮了,猎人的妻子挑起瓦罐去村边井头挑水,但回到半路水就漏完了。这样往返几次,她才发觉瓦罐破了底,生气地回到家门口,抬头一看,倒吸了一口冷气。只见屋檐、门前倒挂着树枝,茅屋四周的地上也被猎人用灶灰团团围着。女鬼既不敢破门而入,也不敢跨越灶灰。她明白猎人已经知道了她的底细,便悻悻离去,再也不来纠缠猎人,而猎人的身体也慢慢地好转。这种赶鬼辟邪的法子后来流传开来,为黎族世代沿用。

## The Custom of the Li People's Hanging Tree Branches Upside Down and Scattering Kitchen Ashes

The Li people have such a custom: any family with a patient at home or having suffered from an abnormal death will hang tree branches upside down in front of their eaves and spread kitchen ashes around their house, in order to drive away ghosts and evil spirits.

According to legend, there was once a man who went hunting with bows and arrows in mountains every day. One day, under a big tree in a deep mountain, the hunter saw a young girl sitting on a stump weaving cloth, whose beauty fascinated him. He stood there still for a long time staring at the girl. Suddenly, the girl turned her head and smiled at him. He seemed to wake up from a dream and plucked up courage to approach her to talk with her. Soon they got acquainted and fell in love, so the hunter took the girl home to live with him.

A few months later, although the couple still loved each other and were happy, the hunter often felt jumpy. His face became sallow; his hands couldn't pull a strong bow; his feet couldn't jump over the mountain river. The former strong young man became skinnier day by day.

One day, on his way back from hunting, the hunter met an old man with grey hair. The old man looked at him for a while and said, "Your wife is a ghost instead of a human being!" The hunter was surprised, but he shook his head with a smile and denied it. "Believe it or not? I'll teach you how to recognize it." The old man whispered and told him something. Then he solemnly said, "Don't let her know. Do what I told you and it can save your life." With these words he went away.

The hunter came home suspiciously and anxiously. He saw his wife greeting him with a smile as usual. That night when they were on bed, the hunter tossed and turned restlessly with a heavy heart. He could not believe that the beautiful wife sleeping beside him was not a human being. "At the first sound of cock crow, you will see…" The old man's words lingered in his ears. That night was very long. In a daze, the first sound of cock crow came from the village. He quickly opened his eyes and looked at his wife. "Ah!" He was so frightened that he almost shouted. Through the moonlight, he saw a white skeleton beside him. When he calmed down, it was strange that his familiar wife was sleeping peacefully beside him. He could no longer fall asleep. Soon, as usual, his wife got up to cook breakfast before dawn. Then he remembered what the old man had said to him: "Your wife was not eating meal but fumigating herself with steam." He crept close to the kitchen, peeping through the cracks in the mud wall. Alas! What the old man had described was true! The fire was dim and in the hazy steam his wife's feet hung on the beam upside down, with her face covered by long dark hair almost soaked in the pot of the boiling porridge. It was so horrible. He didn't dare to look at it any more. He made up his mind to do what the old man had taught him. He quietly smashed several small holes at the bottom of the earthen pot and ran to the hill with a knife. At daybreak, the hunter's wife picked up the earthen pot and went to the village to fetch water from the well. Every time on her half way back, the water would leak out. With several times back and forth, she finally found that the bottom of the pot was broken, so she returned home angrily. When she reached the door, she was astonished to find that branches were hung upside down on the eaves and the door, and the ground around the hut was covered with kitchen ashes. The ghost dared neither break into the door nor cross the kitchen ashes. Realizing that the hunter had known her secret, the ghost went away angrily and never pestered the hunter any more. Gradually the hunter recovered. This way of driving away ghosts and evil spirits was passed down to the Li people from generation to generation.

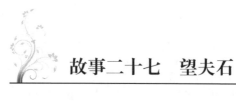

## 故事二十七 望夫石

在霸王岭山脚下,有一个风景秀丽的小村庄,村庄的四周挺立着一簇簇翠绿的椰子树,给这座小村庄增添了许多生气。在霸王岭的山顶上竖立着一座大石头,它活像一个母亲一手抱着一个孩子,一手牵着另一个孩子,在眺望着些什么。村里人把这座石头叫作望夫石。为什么叫它望夫石呢?这里有一个很动人的故事。

很久很久以前,在这个小村子里,有一对年轻的夫妇,男的叫败劳,女的叫伍金,他们男耕女织,相亲相爱,是村里出了名的恩爱夫妻。他们幸福地生活了几年,那位善良又美丽的妻子伍金给丈夫生下一男一女,这真是白糖拌蜂蜜——甜上加甜了。这个小家庭虽然并不富裕,但是随时都可以听到他们那幸福的欢笑声。这是一个多么令人羡慕的家庭啊!

可是好景不长,一个家庭不可缺少的母亲却病倒了,再也起不了床,全村的医生都对她无能为力了。败劳看着病痛难忍的妻子,看着哭喊的孩子们,伤心地流下了眼泪。他发誓一定要把妻子的病治好,重温家庭的欢乐。败劳听说在霸王岭下有一棵兰花仙草,可治百病,但是这座山可不是好对付的,它山势很险,不少人为了摘取兰花草都摔死在山脚下。这些败劳不是不知道,但是为了把心爱的妻子从病魔手中夺回来,他决定上霸王岭去摘取兰花草。当伍金知道丈夫为了她而去冒险的时候,感动得流下了泪,但她不能为了自己而让丈夫去冒险。伍金苦苦地哀求败劳不要去,但是败劳并没有改变他的决定,他信心十足地看了一眼妻子和可爱的孩子们,就匆匆地上路了。

伍金每天都躺在床上默默地为丈夫祈祷着,她希望丈夫能够平平安安地回来。但是,日子一天天过去了,败劳还是没有回来,伍金的病越来越重了。一种不祥之兆始终笼罩着伍金。她再也躺不住了,决定带着两个孩子上山去寻找丈夫,只要能找到日思夜想的丈夫,死也心甘情愿。就这样,伍金带着两个孩子,蹒跚地向霸王岭走去。他们在山上摸索了一整天,才爬上了山顶,但是爬上了山顶却没有找到丈夫的身影。突然,伍金发现在山崖下面有一根树枝钩着一件汗衫。仔细一看,天啊!原来是丈夫的汗衫。"败劳,败劳!"伍金痛苦地呼喊丈夫的名字,她完全明白了,败劳为了她,为了可爱的孩子们,摔死在这无情的山崖下了。孩子们听到妈妈在呼唤爸爸的名字,也跟着喊道:"爸爸,爸爸!"一声声悲呀一声声哀,任凭怎么呼唤,山谷始终只留下一阵阵凄凉的回音。伍金虽然知道败劳已经摔下深深的峡谷,但是她仍然不愿意离开这里,她希望败劳有一天会奇迹般地出现在她的眼前,她要在这里等待败劳的出现。于是,她一手抱着一个女孩,另一手牵着一个男孩,信心十足地站在那里,静静地等待着,盼望着……

一天天过去了,一年年过去了,败劳始终没有出现在他们的眼前,可伍金他们却变成了石头,永远地站在霸王岭的山顶上,眺望着茫茫的山谷……

村里人被她的痴情感动了,他们为了纪念这段令人悲哀的往事,就把这块石头称作望夫石。望夫石的故事便一代一代地流传了下来。

# Wangfushi[①]

At the foot of the Bawangling Mountain, there is a small village with beautiful scenery. Around the village stand rows of verdant coconut trees which add a lot of vitality to the village. On top of the mountain stands a large stone, which looks like a mother holding one child in each hand.

---

① The Husband-waiting Stone.

The villagers call this Wangfushi. Why is it called Wangfushi? Here is a moving story.

Long ago, there was a young couple in this small village. The husband named Bailao and the wife named Wujin. The husband tilled in the field and the wife wove cloth at home. They loved each other very much and were known for their love in the village. After they gave birth to a son and a daughter, their life was really like adding sugar to honey—sweeter and sweeter. Although this small family was not rich, people could always hear their happy laughter. What a lovely family it was!

But their good times didn't last long. One year, Wujin fell ill seriously and could not get up any more. All the doctors in the village were of no help to her illness. Looking at his sick wife and the crying children, Bailao shed tears sadly. He vowed to cure his wife and revive the happy family. He heard that there was a magic orchid on the cliff of the Bawangling Mountain which could cure all kinds of diseases. However, it was not an easy job. Many people who wanted to pick the orchid fell to their deaths at the foot of the mountain. Although Bailao knew all the dangers, he decided to go to the Bawangling Mountain to pick the magic orchid in order to save his beloved wife's life. Knowing that her husband was taking risks for her, Wujin was moved to tears, but she wouldn't let her husband do it. Wujin pleaded with his husband bitterly not to go, but Bailao had made up his mind. He took a confident look at his wife and lovely children and set out.

From then on, Wujin lay in bed praying silently for her husband everyday. She wished that her husband could come back safely. However, as days went by, Wujin's husband did not come back and her illness got worse and worse. An ominous omen hung over her. She couldn't lie down any more and decided to take her two children up to the mountain to search for her husband. If she could find her beloved husband, she would die willingly. So Wujin took her two kids staggering toward the Bawangling Mountain. They spent a whole day climbing up to the mountain top, but did not find her husband. Suddenly, Wujin found an undershirt hanging on a branch of the cliff. She looked at it carefully and found that it belonged to her husband. "Bailao! Bailao!" Wujin cried out her husband's name painfully. She realized that her husband had fallen from the cliff and died. When the children heard their mother calling their father's name, they also cried, "Daddy! Daddy!" No matter how hard they called, the valley left only bleak echoes. Although Wujin knew that Bailao had fallen into the deep valley, she was still reluctant to leave. She hoped that Bailao would miraculously appear one day, and she was willing to wait for Bailao. So holding a girl in one hand and a boy in the other, she stood there confidently, waiting quietly and looking forward.

Day by day and year by year, Bailao never appeared in front of them. Wujin and her children turned into stones, standing on top of the Bawangling Mountain forever, looking at the vast valley.

The villagers were moved by Wujin's love. In order to commemorate this sad story, they called the stone Wangfushi. The story of Wangfushi has been handed down from generation to generation.

## 故事二十八 兄弟俩

很久很久以前，有两兄弟，本是同一个母亲生，却不同一条心。哥哥是一个好吃懒做、性子粗暴的人，弟弟则是一个勤俭耐劳、聪明老实的人。父母双亡后，弟弟经常受到哥哥的虐待。有一次，哥哥提出分家，可是家里穷得很，只有父母遗留下的一头牛和一只猫。哥哥夺去了牛，猫归弟弟。

从此以后，他们就分家，各过各的生活。哥哥天天睡觉到日头晒屁股才牵牛去犁田。弟弟只得抱着猫哭。猫见他哭得很伤心就劝他说："阿弟，你别哭，没有牛犁田你就牵我去当牛吧。"弟弟只好含泪答应。猫很听他的话，好使极了，不用几天就把一片田犁完。哥哥见弟弟的猫比他的牛犁得还快，就想把弟弟的猫夺回来。

有一天，哥哥趁弟弟不在家，就偷偷地把弟弟的猫牵去犁田。可是猫不听他的话，怎样赶、怎么打都不动，气得他鼻孔冒烟，扬起牛鞭狠狠地打，结果把弟弟的猫打死在田里了。

弟弟回来后，见猫死在田里，伤心地放声大哭，哭得非常悲伤，就是山里的鸟儿听到他的哭声都替他掉泪。弟弟把猫埋在田边，天长日久，坟上长出了两棵竹子。

一天中午，弟弟来到坟边竹子旁，忽然刮起一阵风，竹叶纷纷落地，尘土使他睁不开眼。风停了，他睁眼一看，坟地上满是金钱。他又惊又喜，连忙把钱拾回家，买了一头牛，置办了一些家具，生活过得比以前好一些。哥哥见弟弟家境一下变得好起来，感到非常奇怪，就来到弟弟的家想看个究竟，要求弟弟把真相讲给他听。弟弟是个老实人，就从头到尾透露给哥哥。

于是，第二天中午，哥哥也来到坟边竹子旁。一会儿，果然刮起一阵风，竹叶纷纷落地，尘土吹得他睁不开眼。风停了，他睁眼

## 第五章
黎族经典民间故事汉英对照

一看，哪有什么金钱，头上身上全是狗屎！他气得咬牙切齿，憋着一肚子火来到弟弟家大骂一顿，说是弟弟骗了他，并起了坏心，把坟前的两棵竹子砍掉了。

弟弟含泪把竹子拾回家削成小节，织成一个竹筐，里面放些禾草吊在门旁边。一个星期过去了，不管是山鸡、鹧鸪，还是麻雀、黄莺，山里各种鸟都飞来筐里下蛋。弟弟每天早上起来，筐里总是堆得满满的，他不但吃不完，而且拿去卖。

这回又被哥哥的贼眼看见了，可是他不知道弟弟是怎样得来这么多鸟蛋的，感到莫名其妙。他又厚着脸皮到弟弟家里央求弟弟告诉他鸟蛋的来源，弟弟只好告诉了他。于是，哥哥便把弟弟的竹筐拿回他家挂在门旁边。一个星期后，山里的鸟都飞来歇脚，他乐得往筐里一看，里面堆满了鸟屎。他气势汹汹地来到弟弟家大骂一顿，说弟弟又欺骗了他，这下又把弟弟的竹筐烧掉了。

弟弟只好忍气吞声，把哥哥烧掉的筐灰撒到他的田里去种植水稻。他天天早出晚归，辛勤地除草管理，水稻长得非常好，谷子结得很饱满，猪和鸟从不偷吃，他的生活过得越来越好。

哥哥的田里虽然也种上了水稻，可是荒芜得稻和草都难以区分。有一天，哥哥来到田边看他的水稻长得怎么样了，只见一群山猪在里面拱得乱七八糟。他东呼西赶，越赶山猪越凶。一群山猪向他追来，他赶紧逃命。可是，他逃不脱山猪的追击，结果山猪把他团团围住，活活地咬死了。

## The Two Brothers

Long long ago, there were two brothers. Although they had the same parents, they were totally different in characters. The elder brother was lazy and ill-natured, while the younger brother was thrifty, hard-working, intelligent and honest. After the death of both parents, the younger brother was often abused by the elder brother. One day, the elder brother proposed to divide up the family property, but the family was very poor, with only a cow and a cat left by their parents. The elder brother got the cow, and the younger brother got the cat.

From then on, they separated and lived their own lives. Every day the elder brother didn't get up to plough the field until noon, while the younger brother had nothing to do but cry with his cat in arms. Seeing the younger brother crying so sadly, the cat comforted him, "Don't cry, younger brother. You can use me to plough the field as an ox." The younger brother had no choice but to agree with tears. The cat was very obedient and finished ploughing a field in a few days. When the elder brother saw that the cat ploughed the field even faster than his ox, he wanted to snatch the cat.

One day, when the younger brother was out, the elder brother secretly stole the cat to plough his field. But the cat didn't obey his order. No matter how he drove or beat it, the cat just didn't move. He was so angry that he raised the bull whip and beat it hard. As a result, he killed the cat in the field.

When the younger brother came back and saw the dead cat in the field, he cried out so sadly that even the birds in mountains cried after him. Then the younger brother buried the cat in the field. As time went by, two bamboos sprouted up from the grave.

One day at noon, when the younger brother came to the bamboos beside the grave, a gust of wind blew up and the bamboo leaves fell to the ground. The dust made him unable to open his eyes. After the wind stopped, he opened his eyes and found that the grave was covered with gold coins. Surprised and delighted, he quickly picked up the coins and went back home. He used the money to buy a cow and some furniture, and lived a better life. When the elder brother saw the younger brother's life getting better, he felt very strange. He came to the younger brother's home and enquired about the truth. The younger brother was honest and told his elder brother the whole story.

So at noon the next day, the elder brother came to the bamboos beside the grave too. After a while, a gust of wind blew up and the bamboo leaves fell to the ground. The dust rolled in the sky so that he couldn't open his eyes. After the wind stopped, he opened his eyes expecting to see gold coins. But there was no money at all; instead there was shit all over his head! He gnashed his teeth in anger and came to the younger brother's house. He shouted abuse at the younger brother and said that his brother cheated him. Then he cut off the two bamboos beside the grave.

With tears in his eyes, the younger brother picked up the bamboos home, cut them into small pieces, and made a bamboo basket. He hung the bamboo basket beside the door and put some grass in it. A week later, all kinds of birds including pheasant, partridge, sparrow, oriole came to lay eggs in the basket. Every morning when the younger brother got up, he found that the basket was full of bird eggs. There were too many bird eggs for him to eat up, so he could sell some.

Again this was seen by his brother. He wondered how his brother got so many eggs, so he went to the younger brother's home and begged him to tell the secret of the birds' eggs. The younger brother had to tell him. This time the elder brother took his younger brother's bamboo basket back to his home and hung it beside the door. A week later, all the birds in mountains came to rest their feet in the bamboo basket. He was very glad and looked into the basket, only to find bird droppings full of the basket. He came to his brother's home angrily and scolded him, saying that his brother cheated him again, and then burned the bamboo basket.

The younger brother swallowed the insult silently and scattered the ashes of the bamboo basket into his field to nourish the paddy. He worked hard every day to weed. The rice grew very well, without any boars and bird coming to eat it, and his life became better and better.

Although the elder brother's field was also planted with rice, it was so wasted that rice seedlings and grasses could hardly be distinguished. One day, when the elder brother came to the field to see how his rice was growing, he saw a group of boars in the field making a mess. He shouted loudly and tried to drive the boars away, but failed. Even worse, a group of boars chased after him. He had to run for his life, but failed to escape from the attack of the boars. The elder brother was finally surrounded by the boars and bitten to death.

## 故事二十九 色开成家

很早很早以前,有一个孤儿叫色开,从小父母双亡,独自生活,过着清贫的日子。

有一天,色开上山砍柴。路上,他看见一群蚂蚁被山火团团围住,无路可逃。蚂蚁见到色开,就哀求说:"救救我们吧!以后你有什么事,我们会帮助你的。"色开灵机一动,便把一根大木头扛来,架在大火上,蚂蚁们就顺着大木头爬了出来,得救了。

又有一天,色开在湖边看见一伙人在拉网捕鱼,觉得有趣,便坐在湖边观看。忽见一条大鱼向他游来,头露出水面,满脸泪水,向他哀求道:"好心的色开,救救我和我的种族吧!那些狠心的人把我的子孙都捕捉完了,仅留下我一条命,请把我搬到西边那个大湖中去。往后,你有什么事,我可以帮助你。"色开很同情地把它放到西边的大湖中去了。

色开眼下已经快二十五岁了,长得十分英俊,可是姑娘都嫌他穷,不肯嫁给他。邻寨一个奥雅有一个独生女儿,生得十分标致,年约十八。媒婆和小伙子踏破门槛求亲,可是姑娘却没有一个中意的。奥雅也因此而苦恼,便想出一个主意,扬言:"谁能答对和完成我的两件事,谁就当我的女婿。如果答不出和做不到,则要罚三头牛。"许多青年后生都答不出和做不到,被罚了牛。也有一些后生自忖赔不起牛而放弃了。

村里有一个好心人,看到色开善良、聪明,很同情他,愿出三头牛让色开去试一试。起初,色开不想去,后来那个人再三催促他才去了。

奥雅见色开衣服褴褛,不屑地瞟了一眼说:"你也敢来吗?"色开点了点头。奥雅说:"看你这个样子,我不会出太难的问题。"他便吩咐家人把九箩谷子撒在地上，要色开在一天内把这九箩谷子一粒不剩地捡回谷箩里，只要剩下一粒谷子，就要罚牛。色开捡呀捡呀，到了太阳快落山时，才好不容易捡了半谷箩。色开担心起来，自言自语地说："今天收不完谷子，我只好拿人家的牛去赔呢。"他的话被蚂蚁们听见了，蚂蚁纷纷赶来，对色开说："别怕，我们来帮你。"于是，成千上万的蚂蚁涌上去，不一会儿，就把谷子收拾得干干净净，一粒不剩。太阳落山时，奥雅过来一看，满意地点了点头说："这次算你做到了。不过，还有第二件事，你明天一早就去西边湖中寻找我丢失在湖里的衣针，找到后拿给我。"第二天一早，色开就来到了湖边，看见湖水茫茫、深不见底，别说一天难寻到，就是一年也找不到那枚针。于是，他便自言自语地说："这下子三头牛完了。"色开的话被大鱼听到了，它游过来问："色开，你有什么心事？"色开一五一十地说了，大鱼说："色开你莫慌，我们来帮你。"说完，就把鱼子鱼孙招来分头寻找；不一会，这枚小小的衣针便被找到了。色开高兴地拿着针，回去交给奥雅。奥雅也很满意，立即命人击鼓敲锣，当众宣布色开为女婿。色开为得到美丽的姑娘高兴得晕倒在地。当他醒来的时候，发现自己睡在床上，那个美丽的姑娘就在他的身边守着他。从此，他们夫妻恩爱，生活得非常幸福和美满。

不久，奥雅死了，色开继承了遗产，他和妻子把田和牛都分给了穷人，大家都很感激他。

## The Story of Sekai's Getting Married

Long long ago, there was an orphan named Sekai whose parents died when he was a little boy, and he lived a poor life alone.

One day, Sekai went up the mountain to cut firewood. On the way, he saw a group of ants surrounded by mountain fires. There was no way for them to escape. When the ants saw Sekai, they begged, "Save us, please! We'll help you when you need us in the future." Sekai got an idea immediately. He carried a big piece of wood and set it up on the fire so that the ants could climb out of the fire along the big wood. Those ants were saved.

Another day, Sekai saw a group of people fishing by the lake. He found it interesting and sat by the lake to watch them fishing. Suddenly he saw a big fish swimming towards him, with its head above the water and face full of tears. The fish begged him, "Merciful Sekai, please save me and my race! Those hard-hearted people have captured all my descendants, and I am the only one left. Please move me to the big lake in the west. In the future, if you have any trouble and need my help, I will help you." Sekai felt pity for the fish and moved it into the big lake in the west.

At that time, Sekai was about twenty-five years old. Although he was very handsome, no girl would like to marry him because he was very poor. The head of the neighbor village had a beautiful daughter who was about eighteen years old. There were lots of matchmakers and young men coming to make proposals, but the girl didn't like anyone of them. The head of the neighbor village was distressed about this and he came up with an idea. He declared, "Whoever can answer my question and complete my task will be my son-in-law, but he also will be fined three bulls for failure." Many young men tried but could not answer the question or complete the task, and were fined bulls. Some other young men who thought they could not afford the fine gave up.

There was a kind-hearted man in the village who was touched by Sekai's kindness and intelligence, and also had sympathy with Sekai. He was willing to give Sekai a chance to try by providing him with three bulls. At first, Sekai was unwilling to do it. But under the man's repeated urging, he agreed to have a try.

The head of the neighbor village looked scornfully at Se kai's shabby clothes and said, "Do you dare to try?" Sekai nodded his head. The head said, "Seeing you dressed like this, I won't go too far." He ordered his family to scatter nine baskets of millet on the ground and asked Sekai to pick them all up in one day. With one grain left, he would be fined bulls. Sekai picked and picked, but till the sun set, he only finished half basket. Sekai became worried and said to himself, "I can't collect all the millet today, so I have to take other people's bulls to pay for it." His words were heard by the ants. They rushed to him and said, "Don't be afraid. We can help you." Soon, thousands of ants swarmed up and cleaned up the millet, leaving not a single grain on the ground. At sunset, the head came to check. Seeing the result, he nodded with satisfaction and said, "You did it this time. But there's another task for you. Go to the lake in the west early tomorrow morning and find the sewing needle I have lost in the lake. After you find it, bring it back to me." Early next morning, Sekai came to the lake. But when he saw the vast and deep lake water, he was disappointed. One could not even find the needle in a year, not to mention in a day. So he sighed and said to himself, "All three bulls will be gone now." When the big fish heard the words of Sekai, it swam over and asked, "Sekai, what's your trouble?" Sekai told the fish everything. The big fish said, "Don't worry. I can help you." Then the big fish called all its descendants to look for the needle in the lake separately. Soon, the little sewing needle was found. Sekai happily returned to the head with the needle. The head was also satisfied with Sekai. He immediately ordered people to beat drums and gongs to celebrate, and declared Sekai his son-in-law in public. Sekai was so delighted to get the beautiful girl that he fainted to the ground. When he woke up, he found himself lying on bed, and the beautiful girl was beside him. From then on, the couple loved each other and lived happily.

　　Soon after the head of the village died, Sekai inherited his property. He and his wife shared their lands and cattle with the poor, and everyone was grateful to him.

## 故事三十 龟女婿

古时候,在海南岛五指山南开河边,有一个打鱼人,他没有一个晚上不打鱼。回来时,竹篓里总是装满了鱼。除了自己吃,还有剩余晒干存起来。

有一天,太阳刚下山,他就拿着捕鱼网下河去了。说来也怪,偏偏那个晚上他没有打到鱼,连一条小鱼也不进网。每次撒下网,捞上来的都是一只乌龟。捞到半夜,竹篓还是空空的。他没有办法,只好把那只乌龟带回家,给他的女儿玩。他有两个女儿,大女儿名叫贝娓,小女儿叫贝村。贝娓非常讨厌乌龟,贝村却非常喜欢乌龟。

有一天,贝村上山放牛,也把乌龟带去。她和牧童们把牛赶到一个大潭旁边的坡地上后,就坐在绿荫覆盖的厚皮树下玩起乌龟来。别人看见乌龟好玩,就哄贝村去找牛,乘机把乌龟当砖石垒三足灶,用来煮东西。生火时,乌龟感到热,便跑到大潭里去了。贝村把牛赶回来后不见乌龟,就问牧童:"你们看见我的乌龟吗?"大家都装作没有听见,她就一个一个地问。最后问到一个小妹妹,小妹妹如实地把乌龟跑到大潭里去的经过说了出来。

贝村知道后,便沿着乌龟脚印一直跟踪到潭边。这时候,忽然听到潭的对面滴沥滴沥的水响声,她一看,哎呀!一个俊秀的后生哥正在潭边洗头。贝村问:"阿哥喂!看见我的乌龟没有?"后生哥反问:"你为什么要找乌龟呢?"贝村说:"我有一只乌龟不见了。"后生哥听到她这一说,好久好久没有回答。贝村急问:"你到底有没有看见呀?"那后生哥把声音压得很低很低地说:"唉!我没看见!"贝村又问:"人家告诉我,它跑到这个大潭来了,你若看见了,就告诉我吧!"后生哥对贝村说:"如果你真的是找乌龟,我可以告诉你。但你为什么让人用火烧它呢?"贝村说:"哎呀!那是人家害它的,不是我,我疼爱它!"那后生哥听贝村这么一说,觉得她很诚实,就对她说:"如果真的那样,就请你把眼睛闭起来。"贝村毫不犹豫地合上了双眼,顿时听到狂风呼呼,散沙四溅。一会儿,那后生哥叫她把眼睛睁开。哟!一条又宽又直的沙路,从潭的这一头跨过那一头。贝村就从沙路上走过去。到了潭那边,后生哥见贝村心地好,又长得漂亮,贝村见后生哥也生得俊美,便互相表达爱情。后生哥把她带回去,结婚成家了。

这后生就是乌龟。四五年过去了,贝村和乌龟也有了一个女孩,但贝村的父母亲一直都不知道她的下落,以为她早就死了。

有一天,一只白头翁飞来,停在屋前的那棵大榕树上,叫道:"大伯呀大伯,大妈呀大妈,赶快打扫房子吧,你的乌龟女婿要来啦!"贝村母亲不相信。

过了一会儿,又飞来一只乌鸦,大声叫:"啊!啊!请赶快打扫房子吧,你的乌龟女婿要来啦!"贝村母亲觉得很奇怪,也就随意地打扫了一下房子。

不久,果然贝村抱着女孩和乌龟女婿骑着马,一块回到娘家。到了门口,乌龟不下马,一直坐在马背上,村寨的人都好奇地围着观看。看的人,有的指手画脚,有的交头接耳。岳父岳母见女婿到来,非常高兴,宰鸡杀猪来招待他们。岳父岳母请村里的人陪女婿喝酒,可是谁都不肯跟乌龟在一起,都嫌他长得丑。岳父岳母没有法子,只好请一位老婆婆陪他。乌龟不在乎这些,它坐下来,见酒就喝,见菜就吃,一会儿,它感到热起来了,就把身上的乌龟壳脱下来,变成了一个英俊的青年。这可把大家看呆了,都高高兴兴地来向他敬酒。乌龟女婿的英俊,也打动了姐姐贝娓的心。

酒后,乌龟先骑马回家了,留下妻子和女孩。贝村和女儿在娘家住几天后,也准备回夫家。她走的那一天,姐姐贝娓送她走。她争着抱妹妹的女儿。当她们走在杧果树下,发现上面果子累累,贝娓掐了一下女孩的屁股,让孩子大哭起来。她便对妹妹说:"孩子要吃果子，你爬上去摘几个吧！"妹妹信以为真，就爬上树去。当妹妹爬上树时，她悄悄拿出藏在身上的柴刀去砍树。妹妹看见心里一慌，从树上掉了下来，摔死了。姐姐马上换上妹妹的衣服，抱着妹妹的女儿回到乌龟家。

回到妹夫家，乌龟打量了她一番，对她说："你不是我的妻子！"贝娓说："哎呀！你的眼睛瞎了！我不是你的妻子，谁是你的妻子？"乌龟说："你要是我的妻子，就请你从我家所有的米缸中，说出哪个是糯米缸，哪个是粳米缸。"贝娓被难住了。乌龟确信她不是自己的老婆。贝娓又说了好些花言巧语，乌龟还是不相信。

有一天，乌龟的女儿上山收割山兰稻，听到一只鸟在啼叫："我的女儿长大了吗？来照顾照顾我吧！"女儿回家就把听到的话告诉了父亲。乌龟听女儿这么一说，就赶忙跑到山兰园去，对鸟儿说："如果你真的是我的妻子，就飞来停在我的手指上。"他的话音刚落地，那只鸟便飞来停在他的手指上。乌龟把它带回家，煮热饭给它吃，鸟儿吃下热饭，它的羽毛变成了美丽的花衣裳，贝村又复活了。乌龟看见妻子，非常高兴。女儿见了妈妈泪水直流，紧紧地搂住妈妈。

贝村又变成人后，她姐姐再也无法在贝村家待下去，悄悄溜回了娘家。

从此，贝村又和乌龟、女儿生活在一起，过着幸福的生活。

## Turtle Son-in-law

In ancient times, there was a fisherman near the Nankai River in the Wuzhishan Mountain, Hainan Island. He fished every night. Every time he came back, his bamboo basket was full of fish. In addition to the fish for his families to eat, there were remaining fish to be dried and stored.

One day, as soon as the sun set, he went into the river with his fishing net. It was very strange that he couldn't catch any fish that night except for a turtle every time he cast the net. Till midnight the basket was still empty, so he had no choice but to take the turtle home as a gift for his daughters. He had two daughters, the elder one named Beiwei and the younger one named Beicun. Beiwei hated the turtle, while Beicun liked the turtle very much.

One day, Beicun went herding cattle on the mountain and took the turtle with her. After she and the other shepherd boys drove the cattle to the slope beside a big pool, they sat under a lannea coromandelica with deep shade and played with the turtle. Seeing that the turtle was fun, some shepherd boys cheated Beicun to look for cattle so that they could play tricks on the turtle. They used the turtle as a brick base to make a tripod and cook things on it. When the fire was lighted, the turtle felt hot and crept into the big pool. When Beicun drove the cattle back, she couldn't find the turtle. She asked the others if they saw her turtle. Everyone pretended not to hear, so she asked them one by one, and finally a little girl told her the truth.

When Beicun learned that the turtle had crept into the big pool, she followed the turtle's footprints all the way to the pool. At that time, she suddenly heard the sound of dripping water across the pool. Looking ahead, she found a handsome young man washing his hair by the pool. Beicun asked, "Excuse me! Did you see my turtle?" The young man responded by asking, "Why are you looking for a turtle?" "Because I have lost it," answered Beicun. Hearing this, the young man kept silent for a long while. "Did you see it?" Beicun asked urgently. Then the young man lowered his voice and said, "Alas! I didn't see it!" Beicun asked again, "I was told that it came to this big pool. If you have seen it, please tell me!" The young man said, "If you really want to find the turtle, I can tell you. But why did you let someone burn it?" Beicun answered, "Oh, that's some others who harmed it, not me. I love it!"

When the young man heard Beicun's words, he thought she was honest and said, "If that's true, please close your eyes." Without hesitation, Beicun closed her eyes. At once she heard the wind whirring and the sand splashing. After a while, the young man asked her to open her eyes. Oh! She found a wide straight sandy road striding over the pool. Beicun walked along the sandy road to the other side of the pool. When the young man saw that Beicun was both kindhearted and beautiful, he fell in love with her at once. Meanwhile, Beicun also admired the handsome young man. They expressed their love to each other. The young man took Beicun back home, and they got married.

That young man was the turtle. Four or five years later, Beicun and the turtle had a daughter. However, Beicun's parents had never known her whereabouts and thought she had died long ago.

One day, a Chinese bulbul flew into the yard, stopped on the big banyan tree in front of the house and cried, "Uncle, uncle, aunt, aunt, clean the house quickly, as your turtle son-in-law is coming!" Beicun's mother didn't believe it.

After a while, a crow flew in the yard and shouted, "Croak! Croak! Please clean the house quickly. Your turtle son-in-law is coming!" Beicun's mother felt very strange, so she cleaned the house carelessly.

Shortly afterwards, Beicun returned to her parents' home with her daughter and her turtle husband on horseback. At the entrance, the turtle husband did not get down from the horseback so the villagers all watched him curiously, some pointing fingers and others exchanging whispers from ear to ear. The parents-in-law were very happy to see their son-in-law come and cooked chicken and pork to entertain them. The parents-in-law also invited some villagers to drink with the turtle son-in-law, but nobody would like to be with him due to his ugly appearance. The parents-in-law had no choice but to invite an old woman to accompany him. The turtle didn't care about this. He sat down and began to drink and eat at ease. After a while, he felt hot so he took off the turtle shell and turned into a handsome young man. People were astonished to see this and they all toasted him happily. The handsome turtle son-in-law also touched the heart of the sister, Beiwei.

After dinner, the turtle rode home first, leaving his wife and daughter to stay longer. Several days later, Beicun and her daughter were going to return home. On the day she left, her sister Beiwei saw her off. She rushed to carry Beicun's daughter. When they walked under a mango tree and found that it was heavy with fruits, Beiwei pinched the girl's buttock and made her cry, then she said, "The baby wants to eat mango. Why don't you climb up the tree and pick a few?" Beicun believed her words and climbed up the tree. Seeing Beicun up on the tree, Beiwei quietly took out the firewood knife hidden in her clothes and tried to cut down the tree. Beicun was so frightened that she fell from the tree and died. Beiwei immediately put on Beicun's clothes and returned to the turtle's house with Beicun's daughter in her arms.

When Beiwei got to the turtle's house, the turtle looked at her and said, "You are not my wife!" "Oh, dear," said Beiwei, "Are you blind? If I'm not your wife, who is your wife?" The turtle said, "If you are my wife, please tell me which is the glutinous rice jar and which is the japonica rice jar in my house." Beiwei was stumped. The turtle was convinced that she was not his wife. Beiwei said a lot of good words, but the turtle just didn't believe her.

One day, when the turtle's daughter went up to a mountain to harvest the Shanlan rice, she heard a bird crying, "Has my daughter grown up? Take care of me!" When the daughter came home, she told her father what she had heard. When the turtle heard his daughter's words, he rushed to the Shanlan field and said to the bird, "If you are really my wife, fly and stop on my finger." As soon as he finished these words, the bird came and stopped on his finger. The turtle took it home and cooked hot rice for it. After the bird ate hot rice, it turned into Beicun with its feathers turning into beautiful clothes. Beicun revived. The turtle was very happy to see his wife. When the daughter saw her mother, she hugged her mother tightly, with tears rolling down her cheeks.

After Beicun revived, Beiwei could no longer stay at Beicun's home. She had to slipped away to her parents' home.

From then on, Beicun lived happily with her turtle husband and daughter.

## 故事三十一　红蘑菇与白蘑菇

从前有一个穷苦人家的儿子，名叫色开。他父亲死得早，只剩下他和母亲过着贫困的生活。

有一天，母亲叫色开去捉鱼。到了溪边，色开看见一只乌鸦站在一个金黄色的圆圆的南瓜上。他上前赶走了乌鸦，抱起那个大南瓜，带回了家。

色开的朋友看见这南瓜，不由得眼红起来，问色开说："你的南瓜哪里来的？是不是偷人家的？"色开便将得到南瓜的经过告诉了这个朋友。朋友不相信，说："我不相信，这南瓜一定是偷来的，不如将它煮熟，大家吃了吧。"色开不答应，说要留下这个南瓜做种子。

有一天，色开上山砍柴，忽然看见一棵树上长着两朵蘑菇，一朵是红的，一朵是白的。色开摘下那两朵蘑菇，先把红蘑菇放在鼻子上闻了一下。起初，他感到头顶上发痒，接着发热发痛，痛得他倒在地上直爬。一会工夫，他头上冒出一对长长的角来。他一边爬一边叫，鼻子恰巧碰到了那朵白蘑菇。他一闻，头上的角竟缩了回去，头也不痛了。色开高兴极了，便将这两朵奇怪的蘑菇像宝贝一样带回家去。

色开回到家，发现南瓜不见了，就去问他的朋友。到了朋友家，色开看见朋友正准备煮南瓜吃，他要拿回南瓜，可是他朋友不肯交还，还说南瓜是色开偷来的。色开想了一下，便对他朋友说："算了，算了，南瓜算不了什么，我还有更宝贵的东西呢。"他朋友忙追问那更宝贵的东西是什么，要他拿出来瞧瞧。色开便先拿出红蘑菇来，那蘑菇鲜红鲜红的，很讨人喜欢。他朋友接过它，放在鼻子上一闻，头上立刻长出了一对角来。他朋友用手一摸，又惊又急，真不知道该怎么办好。色开对他朋友说："我可以医好你头上的角，但是你要将南瓜还给我。"他朋友只得将南瓜还给色开。色开又拿出白蘑菇来，叫他朋友闻了闻，朋友头上的角立刻缩回去了。

色开将南瓜拿回家去，说要将它留作种子。母亲对他说："开儿，要是现在有饭吃多好呀！"谁料，话刚说完，南瓜里竟冒出了香喷喷、热腾腾的饭菜。从此，色开只要对着南瓜说要什么就有什么，再不愁吃穿了。

村里的财主知道色开有个奇妙的南瓜，就派狗腿子将色开抓来，追问南瓜的来历。色开怎么也不肯说，财主火了，便要将色开处死，色开的妈妈只得流着泪将南瓜交了出来。

色开恨透了财主，他想起那奇妙的蘑菇可以惩罚财主，便带着蘑菇走到财主家里，对财主说："我还有比南瓜更好的东西，就是这美丽的蘑菇。谁要是闻一下，他就会长生不老。"财主看见这美丽的蘑菇，马上心都痒了，眼也花了，恨不得立刻把这蘑菇抢过来，忙答道："好，好！"色开将红蘑菇给财主一闻，财主的脑袋上立刻长出一对毛茸茸的长角来。财主急得跳起来，越跳就越痛，痛得他"哎哟哎哟"直叫。财主老婆和家人都吓得远远地跑开，看也不敢看了。财主只得哀求道："求求你，医好我的双角吧，我什么都愿意给你，南瓜也还给你，只要你医好我……"色开要财主先将南瓜交还，财主只得照办。

色开拿回南瓜后，就和母亲一起搬到很远的地方去了。

那贪婪的财主呢，头上的一双角越来越长了，最后变呀变呀，变成一头大角牛了。

## Red Mushroom and White Mushroom

Once upon a time there was a son of a poor family named Sekai. His father died early, so he and his mother lived in poverty.

One day, his mother asked him to catch fish. At the riverside, Sekai saw a crow standing on a golden round pumpkin. He went forward to chase away the crow, and took the big pumpkin home.

When his friend saw the pumpkin, he became green-eyed. He asked Sekai, "Where is your pumpkin from? Did you steal it?" Sekai told his friend how he got the pumpkin, but the friend didn't believe it. He said, "I do not believe you. This pumpkin must be stolen. You'd better cook it and share with us." Sekai refused, saying that he wanted to leave the pumpkin as seed.

One day, when Sekai went up to the mountain to cut firewood, he suddenly saw two mushrooms growing on a tree, one red and one white. Sekai picked them and smelled the red mushroom. At first, he felt itching on the top of his head, and then he had fever and pain on the head. It was so painful that he fell on the ground crawling. After a while, a pair of long horns sprouted from his head. As he crawled and cried, his nose happened to touch the white mushroom. As soon as he smelled it, the horns on his head retracted and he felt no pain on the head any more. Sekai was very happy and took these two magic mushrooms home.

When he returned home, he found that the pumpkin was missing, so he went to ask his friend. When he arrived at his friend's home, his friend was about to cook the pumpkin for meal. Sekai wanted to take back the pumpkin, but his friend refused to return it and said Sekai had stolen it from others. After thinking about it for a while, Sekai said to his friend, "Well, the pumpkin is nothing. I have something else more precious." His friend asked him what it was and begged him to take it out. Sekai took out the red mushroom, which was bright red and lovely. His friend took it and sniffed it, immediately a pair of horns sprouted from his head. His friend touched it with hands, becoming frightened and anxious. He really didn't know what to do. Sekai said, "I can have your horns retracted, but you must return the pumpkin to me." His friend had to return the pumpkin to Sekai. Then Sekai took out the white mushroom and let his friend smell it. Immediately the horns disappeared.

Sekai took the pumpkin home and said he wanted to keep it as seed. His mother sighed, "My son, if only we had a meal now!" To their surprise, with these words a delicious hot meal sprang out from the pumpkin. From then on, no matter what Sekai wanted, as long as he said it to the pumpkin, he could get it immediately. Sekai and his mother didn't need to worry about their life any more.

When the local rich man heard that Sekai had a magic pumpkin, he ordered his henchmen to catch Sekai and inquired about the origin of the pumpkin. Sekai refused to say anything. The rich man got angry and wanted to kill Sekai. Sekai's mother had to hand over the pumpkin sadly.

Sekai hated the rich man deeply. He remembered that the magic mushroom could punish the local bully, so he took the red mushroom to the rich man's house. He said to the rich man, "I have something else much better than the pumpkin. It is this beautiful mushroom. Anyone who smells it will never grow old." When the rich man saw the beautiful mushroom, he was fascinated by it at once. He was anxious to get the mushroom, so he quickly answered, "Okay, good!" Sekai gave the red mushroom to the rich man. As soon as he smelled it, a pair of long hairy horns sprout from his head. The rich man jumped up in a hurry. But the more frequently he jumped, the more painful he was. He screamed loudly with pain, which frightened his wife and other family members and they all ran away from him. The rich man had to beg, "Please, heal me. I'll give you everything you want, and the pumpkin will be returned to you as long as you heal me." Sekai asked him to return the pumpkin at once, and he had to follow his words.

After taking back the pumpkin, Sekai moved to a far place with his mother.

What about the greedy rich man? His horns grew longer and longer, and finally he turned into a big horned bull.

## 故事三十二 阿勇智斗山神

从前,有一座很高的山岭,半山腰上有一片巨大的枫树林。在枫树林的掩映下,有一个很大的石洞,洞里住着一个万恶的山神。离这石洞约有半里路程的山沟里,有一口清水池,池水凛冽,清澈见底。

每逢夏天,当地农民上山打猎、砍柴,口渴了经常到池边来喝水。那个万恶的山神发现了,便在池里撒了"迷魂药"。从此,凡喝了这池水的人,十有八九会中毒,感到头昏脑涨,意识模糊,找不到回家的路而徘徊在池边。这时,山神便出来抓人了。每年因误饮池水中毒,被山神抓去当妻做妾、为奴做婢的年轻貌美的黎家姑娘不计其数。

有一天晌午,岭脚村青年农民阿勇从地里劳动回来,听说他的新婚妻子阿姑早晨上山拾柴,不见回来。他十分焦急,二话不说,心想:肯定是被山神抓走了。于是,他带着弓箭、尖刀骑马向那座高山疾驰。

"的笃、的笃"的马蹄声,从远而近,惊动了石洞里的山神。山神一时慌了手脚,忙将挂在墙上的一幅山水画摘下,扔向山脚,山水画立刻变成一座高山,山神企图以此把阿勇的来路挡住。可是,性子刚强、敢于藐视一切困难的阿勇面向高山硬是下了马,和马一起一步步朝山顶爬去。登山难,加上天气热,阿勇和他骑的骏马都气喘吁吁,汗如雨淋,汗水把脚下的高山淋湿了。顿时,高山下陷,变为河谷。那个不甘失败的山神,见到一计不成,又施一计。他立刻解下腰带,抛下山脚。顷刻间,阿勇的面前出现了一条巨大的蟒蛇,蛇口张开,像个大洞。阿勇因救妻心切,一时不慎,骑马冲进了蛇肚。当他发现自己连人带马进入了蛇肚时,他想起腰

## 第五章
### 黎族经典民间故事汉英对照

间系的尖刀，便立刻取刀把蛇肚剖开，骑马冲了出去。山神的诡计又落空了。他在慌乱中，只好狠恶地施展最后一计了。他取来一瓢仙水，向被禁在石洞里的十个美女身上泼洒过去，结果，十个美女全变成了石像，个个形貌一样。阿勇骑马奔到石洞门口，下马逐个辨认，却认不出哪个是自己的爱妻阿姑。他陷入了苦闷之中，踌躇着，细辨着。忽然，他发现立在最前头的那尊石像眼泪扑簌簌而落。他再次细辨，认定那正是他的妻子阿姑，便将那尊石像扶上马背，骑马奔下山去。

走呀，走呀，又饿又累。他走到一株大榕树下歇凉时，已近黄昏。他正为如何使这石像变回活人而发愁时，忽见大榕树上空乌云翻滚，狂风骤起。接着，树叶上出现了淅淅沥沥的雨声，豆粒大的水珠从树叶上滴落下来。雨水滴在石像上，石像立刻剥落下一块块石皮来。眨眼间，石像不见了。阿勇面前出现了一个和先前一样秀美可爱的女人，她正是自己的爱妻阿姑。这使他喜出望外。在狂喜中，他不由自主地伸出双手，紧紧地抱住了阿姑。这时，他俩欣喜的眼泪夺眶而出，千言万语，却说不出来。一阵短暂的沉默过后，他俩互相抹干了眼泪，相对而笑，双双下跪，谢过大榕树，便先后跨上马背，向回家的路上直奔而去。

## Ayong Fighting Against the Mountain Demon

Once upon a time, there was a very high mountain. On half way up the mountain, there was a huge maple forest. Covered in the maple trees was a large cave in which lived an evil mountain demon. About half a mile away from the cave, there was a clear pool of water. The water in the pool was cool, clean and clear.

Every summer, the local farmers went hunting animals and cutting firewood on the mountain, when they were thirsty, they would come to drink the clear pool water. When the evil mountain demon discovered that, he sprinkled overpowering drugs into the pool. From then on, nine of ten people who drank the pool water would be poisoned and lost their consciousness. Thus they couldn't find their way home and wandered by the pool. Then the mountain demon would come out to catch them. Every year, countless beautiful young girls of the Li nationality were caught as concubines or slaves by the mountain demon due to drinking the water by mistake.

One day at noon, Ayong, a young farmer in Lingjiao Village, came back from field working. When he heard that his newlywed wife, Agu, went up to the mountain to collect firewood in the morning and did not come back, he was very anxious. He knew that his wife must had been taken away by the mountain demon. So with bows, arrows and sharp knives, he rode off at a gallop towards the mountain.

The clatter of the horse's hoofs from afar shocked the mountain demon in the cave. For a moment, the mountain demon panicked. He took off a landscape painting hanging on the wall and threw it at the foot of the mountain. He immediately turned it into a high mountain in an attempt to block Ayong's way. However, Ayong, who was strong-minded and dared to despise any difficulty, dismounted from his horse and climbed up to the top step by step. The mountain was very steep and it was very hot. Soon both Ayong and his horse sweated profusely and their sweat soaked the mountain under their foot. Suddenly, the mountain began to subside and became a valley. The mountain demon was unwilling to fail so he played another trick. He untied his waistband and threw it down at the foot of the mountain. Instantly, in front of Ayong appeared a huge python with its mouth open like a big hole. Ayong was so anxious to save his wife that he rushed by mistake into the python's belly on horseback. When Ayong found that he and his horse rushed into the python's belly, he remembered the sharp knife tied around his waist.

He immediately used the knife to cut the python's belly open and rode out. The mountain demon's trick failed again. In his panic, he had to play his last trick. He took a gourd ladle of magic water and sprinkled it over the ten beautiful women imprisoned in the cave. As a result, all of the ten beautiful women turned into stone statues with the same appearance. When Ayong reached the gate of the stone cave, he could not recognize which one is his beloved wife Agu. He was stuck in depression and hesitation. Suddenly, he found that the stone statue standing in the front burst into tears. He identified it once again and recognized that she was his wife Agu, so he put the stone statue on the horseback and rode down the mountain.

Ayong rode straight forward for a long time and became hungry and tired. It was almost dusk when he came to rest under a big banyan tree. While he was worrying about how to turn the stone statue back into a living person, he suddenly saw dark clouds rolling and strong wind blowing over the big banyan tree. Then, heavy rain began to patter from the leaves. When the raindrops fell on the stone statue, the stone surface was immediately peeled off. In the blink of an eye, the stone statue disappeared. In front of Ayong was his beautiful and lovely wife Agu. This surprised him. He could not help stretching out his hands and holding her tightly. The couple burst into tears with joy. Although they had thousands of words to say, they finally could speak out nothing. After a brief silence, they wiped each other's tears, smiled at each other, knelt down on their knees to thank the banyan tree, then rode on horseback and went straight home.

## 故事三十三　百兽衣

从前,五指山下有一位姑娘名叫阿娜,她母亲死得早,她与父亲相依为命。阿娜是绣花的好手,她给父亲绣了一个美丽的烟袋,不料被峒官看到了。峒官见烟袋绣得那么好,就开口要。她父亲因为烟袋是女儿精心为他绣的,舍不得,不给。这可把峒官惹恼了,他说:"好,不给烟袋,限你三天之内给我办三件事:一是给我拿来三百只公鸡蛋;二是给我拿来像海水一样多的油;三是给我拿来能把天盖满的布。到时候办不到,你就拿头颅来顶替。"说罢扬长而去。

"天下公鸡哪能生蛋?这真是比登天还难!"老父亲摇头叹息,闷闷不乐。阿娜从地里回来,看见父亲愁眉苦脸,便问道:"爸爸,出了什么事啦?"父亲告诉阿娜,峒官限令三天之内要办到三件事,办不到就要被杀头。阿娜笑道:"请爸爸放心,女儿自有办法对付他。"

三天期限到了,阿娜让父亲在家中安心养神,自己拿着一把尺子、一个瓶子到峒官家去。

峒官看见阿娜登门,喝道:"你父亲怎么不来?"阿娜不慌不忙,答道:"我父亲正在家生孩子,没有空来。"

峒官吼叫起来:"天下哪有男人生孩子的?"

阿娜回答说:"老爷,男人既然不能生孩子,公鸡又怎么能生蛋呢?"

峒官被问得哑口无言。

阿娜拿出瓶子,向峒官说:"老爷要我父亲送来像海水一样多的油,现在我带瓶子来,请老爷量海水到底有多少,我们好按量送来。"

峒官被阿娜驳得束手无策,只好答应免了。

阿娜又拿出尺子，对峒官说："老爷要我父亲送来能把天盖满的布，现在我带尺子来，请老爷量量天，看看到底有多长多宽，我们好如数送来。"

峒官理亏词穷，只好又答应免了。

峒官要阿娜父亲办的三件事，都被阿娜对付过去了。阿娜高高兴兴地回到家里，把事情告诉父亲。父亲笑逐颜开，乡亲们都称赞阿娜聪明伶俐。

峒官碰了钉子，又气又恼。他眉头一皱，又想出了鬼主意：阿娜长得俏，把她娶来做小老婆！他对狗腿子说："是好鸟要在我笼子里养，是好花要在我家中香，没见过姑娘有阿娜那么漂亮，快给我要来当小老婆！"

狗腿子奉命来到阿娜家里，告诉她父亲："峒官老爷看上了美丽的阿娜，要娶她做小老婆，限三天之内送过去。"

阿娜父亲见大难临头，急得吃不下、睡不好，唉声叹气，像害了一场大病一样。阿娜知道了，安慰父亲说："请爸爸放心，我自有办法对付。"

阿娜早已跟青年猎手劳丹好上了，劳丹年轻英俊，身子像椰树一样健壮，眼睛像水晶一样明亮，双手像蜜蜂一样勤劳，胸怀像海洋一样宽广，他总是送打来的猎物给穷苦的乡亲同尝。他约了阿娜到昌化江边去对歌。阿娜去时，劳丹已经等在那里，他一见阿娜，就唱道：

"好花开在高山上，
怨手不长难采到；
阿妹你如一朵花，
恨哥家穷配不上。"

阿娜答道：

"荔枝面粗肚里甜，
阿哥虽穷妹不嫌；
天地相好虹做媒，

我俩相爱心相连。"
劳丹又唱道：
"妹有情，哥有意，
妹是风筝哥是线，
风筝几高线不离。"
阿娜又答道：
"哥有情，妹有意，
网下几深铅都连。"

两人对罢歌，劳丹正高兴得很，不料阿娜告诉他一个坏消息：峒官要娶她做小老婆。他顿时垂下头来，心里又气愤，又难过。阿娜说："相爱要学槟榔树，从头到尾一条心。我们分手以后，你上山去打猎，做成百兽衣，穿着去找我，我们一定能白头到老。"

后来阿娜便被峒官抢去了。但她自从进了峒官家，整天闷闷不乐，从来也不曾笑过一次。峒官给她鹿茸汤喝，她把它洒在地上。峒官给她新筒裙穿，她把它扯成碎片。峒官引她笑，她越发不说不笑，弄得峒官没有一点办法。

一天一天过去了，阿娜还是不说不笑，后来索性不吃不喝。峒官急得团团转，派人去问她到底为什么，怎样才能使她高兴。

阿娜说："要是能看见穿百兽衣的人唱歌跳舞，我才会高兴。"
于是峒官到处张贴告示，重金收买百兽衣。

阿娜被抢走后，劳丹跑遍深山密林，打到一百只野兽，剥了兽皮，做成了百兽衣。这天，他穿着百兽衣来到峒官家门前。他边跳边唱道：

"鹿恋故园鸟恋窝
不知亚妹可想哥？
亚哥想你日消瘦，
眼泪如泉流成河。"

阿娜听到歌声，立刻答道：
"哥想妹妹妹想哥，

有情不怕杀命刀,

亚哥如是一只鸟,

妹愿为你来做窝。"

阿娜跑出门口,看见劳丹穿着百兽衣来了,也高兴地笑着跳起舞来。峒官看见了,问阿娜:"你为什么那样喜欢百兽衣?"

阿娜笑道:"百兽衣真好看,谁穿了,谁就招人喜欢。"

峒官听她这么一说,急忙命令劳丹脱下百兽衣,与自己对换。一等两人换好衣服,阿娜就示意劳丹击鼓发令。

劳丹懂得阿娜的意思,就"咚咚"击起鼓来。差役狗腿子一听,是峒官升堂,就急忙过来,只见"峒官"怒气冲冲地喝着:"快把那穿兽衣的野人拉出去斩了!快!快!"狗腿子不分青红皂白,就把穿着百兽衣的峒官杀了。

阿娜和劳丹就高高兴兴地回到村里,和父亲一起过上了幸福的生活。

## Clothes Made of a Hundred Beasts' Skins

Once upon a time, there was a girl named Ana at the foot of the Wuzhishan Mountain. Her mother died early and she lived with her father. Ana was good at embroidering. She embroidered a beautiful tobacco pouch for her father. Unexpectedly, it was seen by the local official who was fascinated with the beautiful tobacco pouch and wanted to own it. Ana's father was reluctant to give it to him because it was attentively embroidered by his daughter. This annoyed the local official. He said, "You do not want to give the tobacco pouch to me. Okay! I order you to do three things for me in three days: first, bring me 300 cock's eggs; second, bring me as much oil as sea water; third, bring me enough cloth that can cover the sky. If you can't do such things in time, you will be sentenced to death." With these words he went away.

"How can a cock lay eggs in the world? It's really harder than flying to the sky!" The old father shook his head and sighed. When Ana came back from the field, she saw her father's sad face. She asked, "Dad, what's wrong with you?" Her father told her what had happened. Ana said with a smile, "Don't worry, daddy! I can deal with him."

When the three-day deadline came, Ana let her father rest at home and she went to the official's house with a ruler and a bottle.

When the official saw Ana coming, he asked why her father did not come. Ana answered calmly, "My father is giving birth to a baby at home. He has no time to come."

The official stormed, "How can a man give birth to a child in the world?"

Ana answered, "My Lord, since men can't give birth to baby, how can cocks lay eggs?"

The official was dumbfounded and didn't know how to answer.

Ana took out the bottle and said to the official, "My Lord, you asked my father to bring you as much oil as sea water. Now I bring the bottle. Please measure the amount of sea water so that we can send oil to you in the same quantity."

The official could do nothing but to exempt her father from it.

Then Ana took out the ruler and said to the official, "My Lord, you asked my father to send you the cloth that can cover the sky. Now I bring the ruler. Please measure the sky to see how long and wide it is. Then we can send cloth to you in the same quantity."

The official had nothing else to do but exempt his father from the task too.

All the three impossible tasks had been done by Ana. She happily returned home and told her father about it. Her father was very happy and the villagers all praised Ana for her cleverness.

However, the local official was very angry and annoyed after his plan bit the dust, so he racked his brain and came up with a wicked idea. He was attracted by Ana's beauty and wanted Ana to be his concubine. He ordered his henchmen, "Good birds are to be raised in my cage, and good flowers are to be perfumed in my home. I haven't seen a girl as beautiful as Ana, so catch her here to be my concubine!"

The henchmen came to Ana's home and told her father, "Our Lord has taken a fancy to the beautiful Anna and wants to take her as his concubine. You must send her to the Lord's house within three days."

Ana's father was so worried about it that he couldn't eat or sleep well. He sighed all day long as if he had suffered a serious illness. Ana comforted her father, "Don't worry, Dad. I have my own way to deal with it."

Ana had fallen in love with a young hunter named Laodan. Laodan was handsome, with a strong figure like a coconut tree and eyes as bright as crystal. He was also very industrious and generous. He often shared his prey with the poor fellow countrymen. That day, he invited Ana to go to the Changhuajiang River to sing antiphonal songs. When Ana arrived, Laodan was already there. As soon as he saw Ana, he began to sing a song,

"Beautiful flower blossoms on high mountains.

I cannot pick it without a long arm.

My beloved is like a flower.

I cannot match you without enough property."

Ana answered with the following song,

"Litchi with course skin is sweeter;

My beloved though poor is not disliked.

Heaven and earth being good matchmakers,

We love each other with hearts together."

Laodan sang again,

"You and I are in love with each other.

You are like a kite and I a thread.

Kite and thread are inseparable forever."

Ana replied again,

"You and I are in love with each other,

Like lotus root fibers connecting forever."

Laodan was very happy after singing the songs when suddenly Ana told him the bad news that the local official wanted to take her as his concubine. He bowed his head and felt angry and sad. Ana said to him, "We should learn how to love each other from betel nut tree, being of one mind from the beginning to the end. After we parted, you go up to the mountains to hunt a hundred beasts and sew a piece of clothing with their skins, and then wear it to find me. We will certainly be together forever."

Soon after Ana was taken away by the official. Since she entered the official's home, she had been depressed every day and never laughed once. The official gave her deer antler soup to drink, but she sprinkled it on the ground. The official gave her a new skirt to wear, but she tore it into pieces. The more the official coaxed her to laugh, the less she talk or smile, which made the official helpless.

Day after day Ana did not laugh or talk, and even did not eat or drink. The official was very anxious so he sent someone to ask her the reason.

Ana said, "I would be happy if I could see a person who wear clothes made of a hundred beasts' skins singing and dancing."

So the official had announcements put up everywhere, which said clothes made of a hundred beasts' skins would be bought at high price.

After Ana was taken away by the local official, Laodan hunted everywhere in mountains and forests. He killed one hundred beasts, removed their skins and sewed them into a piece of clothing. On that day, he came to the door of the official's house in the clothes made of beasts' skins. He danced and sang,

"Deer miss their native place and birds miss their nests,

So I wonder if my beloved misses her lover.

I became emaciated due to missing her,

With tears flowing like springs into river."

When Ana heard the song, she immediately answered with a song,

"The lovers miss each other.

Love is not afraid of killing knives.

If my beloved is a bird,

I am willing to be your nest."

Ana ran out of the door and saw Laodan coming in a beasts' skin clothing. She also laughed and danced happily. When the official saw it, he asked Ana, "Why do you like beasts' skin clothing so much?"

Ana said with a smile, "The clothes made of a hundred beasts' skins is so beautiful. Whoever wears it will be attractive."

Hearing Ana's words, the official urgently ordered Laodan to take off the beasts' skin clothing and exchange it with his official's robe. As soon as they exchanged clothes, Ana signaled Laodan to beat the drum.

Laodan understood Ana's meaning and beat the drum. As soon as the henchmen on duty heard the beating drums, they thought that the local official wanted to hold the court trial, so they hurriedly rushed in. Laodan, the fake official, ordered them angrily, "Pull the wild man in beasts' skin out and chop his head off! Hurry up! Hurry up!" Thus the henchmen killed the local official wearing beasts' skins mistakenly.

After that, Ana and Laodan returned to the village and lived a happy life with her father.

# 故事三十四　聪明的媳妇

从前，有一个心肠恶毒的黎头①，名叫亚厉。他为人刁蛮、狡猾，他家的田地耕不尽，他家的耕牛使不完，这一切都是他"吃"来的。他"吃"人的方法多得很，可是，谁也不敢惹他。

有一天，他骑着大白马看见路边的一块良田，便皱了皱眉，想出坏主意来要"吃"掉这块田。他把白马放进田里吃稻谷后，便和打手们躲进树林里去了。

这块田的主人是一个叫亚实的穷老人，当他看到大白马在自己的田里吃稻谷的时候，就跳进田里赶马。赶来赶去，白马还是转在田里吃稻谷。他生气了，就出尽全部的力气用石头掷过去，刚巧打中大白马的头，大白马顿时惊骇地跳出稻田。

这时，亚厉和打手们气势汹汹地来到老人的面前大声骂道："哈嚩，你是生吞蛇胆了？怎么敢打我的马，唔？"

老人碰到这个恶棍，不知怎样才好，只得胆怯地回答说："你……你的马吃、吃我的稻谷……"

"我的马是金马宝马，光它的两只角就能顶上这块田和田里的稻谷呢！"亚厉指着马头恶狠狠地说："你看，把宝马角打落了……哼！三天之内给我找回来，要不，用你这块田顶上。"说完，牵着白马扬长而去。

可怜的老人望着他们的身影，半天也说不出一句话来。他知道，天底下哪匹马会像牛一样长出两只角来呢？明明是为了"吃"掉他这块田而施的诡计嘛！

他回到家里整天闷闷不乐，愁眉苦脸，连饭都不想吃。他的儿

---

① 即峒首，过去黎族氏族或部族的首领。

媳妇叫亚花，见到这般情景，便奇怪地问："阿公，什么事把你愁成这个样子呢？"老人长长地叹了一口气，然后，一五一十地把事情发生的全部经过讲了出来。

亚花听完后，便安慰他说："不要难过，儿媳有一个好办法。"说完，就在老人的耳边嘀咕了一阵。

第二天，亚实带着儿子到田坑里去用戽斗捉鱼，他们捉到了很多又肥又大又光滑的泥鳅，把大泥鳅拿回家里用木条串成一大串，高高地吊挂在家门前，过路的人赞叹不止。

第三天，亚厉果然带了打手牵着大白马傲慢而得意地来到亚实家门前，一见了一大串黄灿灿、又肥又大的泥鳅，个个口水直流，纷纷呼叫起来："哗，哪里抓了这么多的泥鳅哟？"

"这泥鳅可肥大了，呼呀！"

"哈，把它斩成一节节来炒，配上山兰酒慢慢地喝，就是老婆死了，那也心甘啰！"亚厉叫得更凶更欢。他们空吞了大口口水后，便大叫亚实出来。

老人不慌不忙地走出家门来，亚厉大声对老人说："亚实，你找到我的宝马角吗？"老人摇摇头说："没有……"

"唔，没有找着？"亚厉声嘶力竭地叫道："好，罚你把那块田抵上。算是可怜你，田里的稻谷归你收了，田是我的。"

这时，亚花走出来上前对亚厉说："哟！是亚厉大奥雅！是来催宝马角的吧？"

"是呀！是呀！"打手们齐呼叫起来。

"哎！我阿公打落了你的两只角是应该赔田。"亚花心平气和地说："不过，你们的嘴也太不干净了，你们刚才那一阵呼叫，把我们晒的那串宝鳅的鳞给吹飞了。是不是你们的过错？你们也要给我们找回来，要不，我们决不赔田！"

这一席话，使亚厉和打手们惊得半呆。过了一会，亚厉才鼓大双眼恶狠狠地说："你是喝了生酸竹笋水了？自古以来，泥鳅哪有长鳞的？你……你怎么嘲弄我？唔？"

这时，凑热闹的人们围上来了，亚花趁这个时机回驳说："哈哈，既然你们说泥鳅自古没有鳞，我也听说自古以来马是没有角的。你问过天下的人，哪一个见过生角的马？再说，你的马角是长在肚皮下呢？还是长在屁股上呀？"

"哈……"人群中爆发出一阵嘲笑声。

"这……嘿……"亚厉想不到这个女人竟在众人面前奚落他，而他又拿不出什么道理来答辩，又不好在众人面前发怒，只好牵着大白马，垂着脑袋，在众人的笑声中，像一头斗败的野牛般溜走了。

## The Story of a Clever Daughter-in-law

Once upon a time, there was a wicked head of the Li village named Yali. He was both rude and cunning. He had too many farmlands to be plowed and too many cattle to be used, all of which were got by blackmailing other people. He had many ways to blackmail people, but nobody dared to offend him.

One day, when he rode a white horse on the road and saw a good field, he came up with a bad idea to get it. He drew the white horse into the field to eat rice seedlings, while he and his followers hid in the woods.

The owner of that field was a poor old man named Yashi. When he saw the white horse eating rice seedlings in his field, he came to drive the horse away. However, no matter how he herded it back and forth, the white horse was still turning around to eat rice seedlings in the field. Being very angry, he threw a stone with all his strength at it and hit it on the head. The white horse was shocked and jumped out of the paddy field in horror.

At this time, Yali and his followers came to the old man fiercely and shouted, "Aha! Did you swallow the snake gall? Otherwise how dare you hit my horse?"

Meeting this scoundrel, the old man didn't know what to do, so he had to answer timidly, "Your horse ate my rice seedlings."

"My horse is as precious as gold and its two horns are as expensive as both this field and the rice in the field!" Yali pointed at the horse's head and said fiercely, "Look, you've knocked down my precious horse's horns! Get them back for me in three days, or you must pay me with this field." With these words, he led the white horse away.

The poor old man watched their backs and could not say a word quite a while. He knew that was Yali's trick to get his field because there is no horse growing two horns like a cow in the world.

After he returned home, he was depressed all day long and didn't want to eat anything. His daughter-in-law Yahua saw this and asked him curiously, "Dad, what made you so sad?" The old man let out a long heavy sigh, and told her all about what had happened.

After hearing the story, Yahua comforted him, "Don't worry, dad, I have a good idea." Then she whispered her plan in the old man's ear.

The next day, Yashi and his son went to the pool to catch fish. They caught a lot of big and fat loach. Then they strung those loach with a big stick and hung them high in front of their house. All the passers-by were amazed.

On the third day, as expected, Yali came to Yashi's house arrogantly with his followers and the white horse. When they saw the bunch of yellow, big and fat loach hanging there, they all drooled and called out, "Wow, where did you catch so many loach?"

"The loach are so fat, hoo!"

"Ha, cut them into pieces to stir-fry and then drink with Shanlan rice wine slowly, this will be the sweetest thing in the world, compensating for the death of my wife!" Yali shouted more fiercely. After they had swallowed their saliva in vain, they shouted Yashi out.

The old man went out of his house unhurriedly. Yali shouted to the old man, "Yashi, have you found the horns of my precious horse?" The old man shook his head and answered, "No."

Yali shouted hoarsely and exhaustively, "Well, since you didn't find the horns, your field will be mine to compensate for my loss. To show my pity for you, I allow you to harvest this time's rice."

At this moment, Yahua came out and said to Yali, "Yo! It's master Yali! You are here for the horns of the precious horse, right?"

"Yes! Yes!" The followers shouted together.

"Ah! My father-in-law knocked down your horse's two horns and should definitely pay for that with the land," Yahua said calmly, "But your mouths are too dirty. Your loud shouts just now blew away the scales of my precious loach that we were drying. Isn't it your fault? You should also find them for us; otherwise, we will never pay for your horns!"

These words shocked Yali and his followers. After a while, Yali said fiercely with widened eyes, "You must have drunk the sour bamboo shoot water. Otherwise, how can you mock me in this way? Who have seen the loach scales since ancient times?"

At this time, people gathered around them. Yahua took the opportunity to retort, "Haha, since loach has no scales from ancient times till now, horse has no horns either. Have you ever met anyone who has seen a horned horse in the world? Besides, do your horse's horns grow under its belly or on its buttocks?"

"Ha, ha, ha…" A burst of laughter broke out in the crowd.

"It's… well…" Yali could not have imagined that the woman would ridicule him in public, and he could not think of any reason to debate.

What's more, he could not even get angry in public. As a result, he had to slope off with his white horse and followers in the laughter of the crowd, bowing his head like a defeated buffalo.

## 故事三十五 水与火的故事

远古时候,水与火是一对十分要好的朋友。它们各自都不肯暴露出自己的弱点,互相尊重又互相妒忌。

有一次,火不小心触犯了水,并四处扬言要煮干水。这样,便捅到了水的弱处。于是,水被激怒了。火把大片大片的森林和荒草燃烧起来,连露水也被煮干涸了。后来,火得意扬扬地自夸起来,认为自己是无敌的英雄。

水也不示弱,便联合了大大小小的沟、塘、河、湖的水,向漫天大火冲过去。火挡不住这滔滔大水的进攻,连忙后退。水乘胜追击,把火追得无处躲藏。眼看火将要被湮灭,火王急中生智,便对残火们说:"钻进石块木头,保住火种。"于是,火便迅速地钻进木头和石块,躲过一场灭绝性的灾难。

所以,人们现在能从木头和石块中钻出火来。据说那是那次大战的"幸存者"呢!

## The Story of Water and Fire

According to legend, in ancient times Water and Fire were very good friends, but neither of them was willing to expose their weaknesses. They respected and envied each other.

On one occasion, Fire accidentally offended Water and threatened to boil away the water all over the world, which hit the only weak point of Water and also enraged Water. Fire burned vast areas of forests and weeds, and even dried up every drop of dew. Later, Fire boasted proudly that he was an invincible hero.

Water didn't show weakness at all. He united the water of rivers, ditches, lakes and ponds of all sizes to rush toward the big fire. Fire could not resist the attack of the torrential water and quickly retreated. Water continued to chase Fire and made it nowhere to hide. Seeing that all the fire was going to be annihilated, the Fire King hit on a good idea in emergency. He said to the remnants of the fire, "Worm into stones and woods to keep alive." As a result, the remnants of the fire quickly wormed into the woods and stones, and escaped the devastating disaster.

So even now fire still can be made by drilling woods and stones. It's said to be the remnants of the fire in that battle.

## 故事三十六　哥喂鸟

在五指山区，每到傍晚，人们常会听见一种鸟的啼叫声：哥喂！哥喂！……从山南叫到山北，如诉如泣，听了叫人掉泪。这种鸟名叫"哥喂鸟"，是一个名叫阿香的姑娘变的。她在寻找、呼唤自己的爱人巴昌。

阿香和巴昌是天生的一对，从小就在一起劳动，一起成长。木棉花开了十八次，他俩都长大成人了。巴昌是打猎的能人，阿香是织布的好手，巴昌常给阿香送野味，阿香常给巴昌织寒衣，两人深深地相爱着。有一年的"三月三"，巴昌和阿香游山对歌时，巴昌唱道：

"感谢亚妹一片心，
叫哥怎能答妹情，
缸里没有过夜米，
袋里没有半分钱。"

阿香唱道：

"哥妹同是苦命人，
患难之交恩爱深，
哥是针来妹是线，
穿在一起不断情。"

他们正玩得欢，当时峒主家的少爷来游山，发现阿香长得像仙女一样漂亮，涎水直流，他抱起阿香就要亲嘴，被阿香"啪啪"打了几巴掌。巴昌也怒不可忍，一拳把少爷打个四脚朝天。少爷怀恨在心，逃回家去跟家中打手暗定计谋。

一天清晨，巴昌像往常一样上山去打猎，阿香送了一程又一程。

阿香唱道：

"千里岭来万重山，

送哥越远心越乱，

摘朵鲜花送亚哥，

看花当见妹面颜。"

巴昌唱道：

"一步低来一步高，

碰着石头跌一跤。

跌跤不是脚无力，

心想妹妹才绊脚。"

他俩你唱我和，不觉路远。阿香一直把巴昌送了十八里路才分手。

巴昌在山上打猎，突然雷雨交加，他跑进山洞中躲雨。这时，峒主少爷派来的打手蜂拥而至，对洞中连放几枪，把巴昌打死在洞中，又用大石头堵住洞口。

天黑了，阿香看不见巴昌归来，依门眺望，却只见峒主的少爷带着打手前来抢亲。阿香宁死不屈，拼命挣扎，她一边喊着"哥喂！哥喂！"，直往高山上跑。打手们紧追不放，当阿香跑到山顶时，发现无路可逃，眼看打手快要追上，便毅然从悬崖纵身一跳，以死殉情。打手追到山顶时，只见一只鸟儿展翅从悬崖下面飞起，声声叫着"哥喂！哥喂！"，飞过一山又一山。这只鸟就是阿香变成的，她一直在寻找、呼唤着自己的情人巴昌。

## The Gewei Bird

In the Wuzhishan Mountain area, people often hear the "Gewei! Gewei!" crying of a kind of bird in the evening. The crying of the bird spreads from the south to the north of the mountain area, touching people's heart. The bird is called the Gewei Bird. People said that the bird was transformed by a girl named Axiang who was looking and calling for her lover Bachang.

According to legend, Axiang and Bachang were made for each other. They had worked together and grown up together since they were very young. Bachang was a capable hunter, and Axiang was good at weaving cloth. Bachang often sent game to Axiang, and Axiang often made clothes for Bachang. Gradually, they were deeply in love with each other. At one year's Double Third Festival, Bachang and Axiang climbed up the mountain together and sang love songs to each other.

Bachang sang to Axiang,

"Thank you my lover.

But how can I repay your love,

Since there is neither much rice in my jar,

Nor money in my pocket."

Axiang answered with a song,

"Although we are poor,

We love each other deeply;

You're like a needle and I'm a thread,

Never break when pierced together."

They were having a good time when the son of the village chief came. When the young master found that Axiang was as beautiful as a fairy, he drooled over her. He came near Axiang and wanted to kiss her, but he was slapped several times by her. Bachang was also furious and punched the young master. With a grudge in his heart, the young master fled back home to make a secret plan with his henchmen.

Early one morning, Bachang went hunting in a mountain as usual, and Axiang sent him off for a long way.

Axiang sang to Bachang,

"The mountain road winds treacherously;

The farther away you are, the more confused I am;

Let me pick a flower and send it to my lover;

When you see the flower, you'll see me."

Bachang replied with a song,

"One step high and one step low,

Unconsciously I fall against a stone.

Falling down is not due to weakness,

But because of missing you."

They lost themselves in singing without noticing that they had gone a long way. They had walked eighteen miles before separated.

Bachang was hunting on the mountain when suddenly there was a thunderstorm. Bachang ran into a cave to take shelter from the rain. At that time, the henchmen sent by the young master swarmed in. They shot at Bachang in the cave and killed him. What's more, they blocked the entrance of the cave with a big stone.

When it was dark, Bachang was still not back. Axiang became worried and looked out of the door, only to see the young master of the village chief coming to catch her with his henchmen. Axiang would rather die than surrender, so she struggled desperately. She shouted "Gewei[①]! Gewei!" and ran straight up to the mountain. The henchmen chased after her closely. When Axiang ran up to the top of the mountain, she found no way to escape. Seeing that the henchmen were about to catch up with her, she desperately jumped off the cliff and died. When the henchmen got onto the top of the mountain, they saw a bird flying from the bottom of the cliff to the mountain top crying, "Gewei! Gewei!" The bird was transformed by Axiang who has been looking for her lover Bachang.

---

① It means my lover.

## 故事三十七　捉弄财主

孟征盗富济穷出了名,有钱的财主恨透了他,但孟征偷得巧妙,神不知鬼不觉,又没有什么把柄给人抓在手里,因而财主们对他无可奈何。一天,附近的一个大财主对孟征说:"听人家说你很会偷东西,我家有一只羊,要是你能偷走,那就算我输给你,要是偷不走,哼……"财主用鼻孔打了个哼哼。

孟征知道这是财主故意想办法要整治他,寻思片刻,他想出了个妙计,欣然答应了财主提出的条件,说:"好吧,如果偷不走你的羊,我就给你当一辈子长工。"

条件讲妥。当天夜晚,财主为了不让孟征真的把羊偷走,趁人不注意,特地悄悄地把羊从羊栏里牵到后山坡,缚在深山里。孟征早就料到了这一着,半夜里,他走到财主家的外面学羊挠痒的样子用屁股擦围墙。果然不出所料,孟征擦围墙的声音惊动了财主两公婆。财主婆有些不放心地问财主公:"你把羊缚在那里,是不是绳索断了,羊走回家来了?"

"我缚在后山坡酸豆树头。缚了三条索,断不了。"

孟征站在外面听得清清楚楚,一会儿,便走到后山坡把羊牵去杀了。杀了羊后,他把羊肚放到睡在床上的两个财主女儿中间,羊头放进火塘里,羊尿脖吊在财主公的脖子上,羊肠吊在门楣上,羊皮铺在大门口。他还把大饭锅倒过来盖在门前的垃圾堆上,饭盆翻过来放在屋角。睡到半夜,财主的两个女儿碰到湿漉漉、软绵绵的羊肚便嚷了起来,姐姐说妹妹生了孩子,妹妹说是姐姐生。两人争吵不休,吵得地主婆睡不着觉,便说:"你们别吵了,等我点火看看。"财主婆爬下床来,看见火塘里有两颗闪光的火星。她走到火塘边蹲下来吹火,一蹲下身,头就碰了羊角,痛得她"哎哟,哎哟"地乱叫。财主公听见财主婆喊叫,以为出了什么事,忙爬起身来。他从床上坐起来一下子就摸到了吊在脖子上的羊尿脬,愤怒地说:"你不死我死了,我的尿脬走上脖子了。"

财主公走到门口,摸到了挂在门楣上的羊肠,以为是毒蛇,嚷着说:"哪来这么多毒蛇呀?"他举起木棒朝羊肠乱击,谁知把满屋子的饭碗、菜盘打得稀巴烂。走出门口,他一脚踩在羊皮上,摔得四脚朝天。财主公气了一肚子火,骂道:"这两只死狗都到哪里去了。"他看见垃圾堆上黑乎乎的乌饭锅以为是黑狗,便一棒打去,只听见咣当一声响,锅破了。他转头看见屋角的饭盆,以为是白狗,又一棒打去,盆也破了。

第二天早晨,财主爬起床来,看见满屋子的羊皮、羊肚、羊角……知道上了孟征的当。财主找到了孟征,对他说:"我还有一只鸡,要是你今夜偷去,我永远服你;如果偷不走,送你到县里严办。"孟征笑眯眯地点点头。当天夜里,财主两公婆吸取了前夜的教训,他们坐在火塘旁轮流抱着鸡。男的抱了一会儿又交给女的抱,就这样反复交换,一直挨到了后半夜。他俩抱鸡的情景,被躲在屋顶上的孟征看得一清二楚。当鸡啼第三轮时,孟征看见财主两公婆都打盹了,便从屋顶上抱着一只鸭沿着吊绳爬下来,悄悄地站在他们身后见机行事。当财主公闭着眼睛把鸡交给财主婆时,孟征急忙把带来的鸭塞给财主婆,却把鸡拿走了。

财主婆把鸭抱了一会儿,摸着鸭的嘴巴,闭着眼睛问财主公:"怎么鸡的嘴是扁的?"财主公也困得睁不开眼睛,装得蛮有把握地说:"鸡嘴扁是要啼了。"

早晨醒来,财主两公婆看见手里抱着的是一只鸭,才知道鸡被孟征换去了。

## Meng Zheng Playing a Trick on the Rich Man

Meng Zheng was famous for robbing the rich to help the poor, so the rich people hated him very much. However, Meng Zheng was so clever that he stole things without anyone knowing it, and no evidence was found, so there was nothing the rich people could do about him. One day, a rich man nearby said to Meng Zheng, "It is said that you are very good at stealing. I have a sheep. If you can steal it, it will belong to you; otherwise, you will be punished." The rich man snorted.

Meng Zheng knew that the rich man deliberately tried to punish him, so he thought for a moment and came up with a good tactic. He readily agreed to the terms proposed by the rich man and said, "Well, I'll be your laborer all my life if I can't steal your sheep."

They concluded a transaction. To prevent Meng Zheng from stealing the sheep, the rich man stealthily led the sheep from the sheep pen to the back of the mountain and tied it to a tree there that night. Meng Zheng had expected this before hand. In the middle of the night, he went outside the rich man's house to rub the fence with his buttocks like the sheep tickling. As expected, the sound of Meng Zheng rubbing the fence alarmed the rich man and his wife. The wife asked the rich man uneasily, "You had tied the sheep there. Did the rope break and the sheep come home?"

"I have tied the sheep to the sour bean tree on the back of the mountainside. I tied it with three ropes which can't be broken."

Meng Zheng stood outside and heard clearly. After a while, he went to the back of the mountainside and killed the sheep. He put the sheep tripe on bed between the two sleeping daughters of the rich man, the sheep's head in the Chinese fireplace, the sheep's bladder around the rich man's neck, the sheep's intestines dangling from the lintel, and the sheep skin on the floor of the gate. Furthermore, he put the big rice pot upside down on the garbage heap in front of the door, and the rice bowl bottom up in the corner of the house. In the middle of the night, when the two daughters in their sleep touched the wet and soft sheep belly, they were shocked and shouted. The elder sister said that the younger sister might have given birth to a baby, while the younger sister said that the elder sister might have given birth to a baby. They quarreled so loudly that their mother was disturbed. She said, "Stop quarreling and wait for me to light the fire." The woman got out of bed and saw two sparks shining in the Chinese fireplace. She went near and wanted to blow up the fire. As soon as she squatted down, her head bumped into the sheep's horn and got hurt, so she yelled horribly. Hearing the yelling, the rich man got up to see what had happened. But unconsciously his hand touched the bladder hung around his neck, and he shouted angrily to his wife, "Don't yell any more. My bladder is displaced on my neck."

The rich man went to the door and touched the sheep's intestines hung on the lintel. He mistook them for poisonous snakes and shouted, "Why were there so many poisonous snakes?" He raised a stick to hit the sheep's intestines, only to hit the bowls and dishes into pieces. When he walked out of the door, he stepped on the sheep's skin and fell over. The rich man was very angry and scolded his two dogs. When he saw the black pot on the garbage heap, he mistook it for the black dog, so he hit it with a stick, and the pot was broken. When he saw the rice basin in the corner, he mistook it for the white dog. He hit it again, and the basin was broken too.

The next morning, when the rich man got up and found his room full of sheep skin, tripes and horns, he realized he had been fooled by Meng

Zheng. The rich man found Meng Zheng and said to him, "I also have a rooster. If you can steal it tonight, I will be convinced forever. Otherwise, I will send you to the county yamen to have you punished." Meng Zheng nodded with a smile. That night, the rich man and his wife learned the lesson from the night before. They sat by the Chinese fireplace and took turns to hold the rooster. After the husband held the rooster for a while and felt tired, he gave it to the wife. In this way they took turns on duty until the small hours came and both of them were very sleepy. Hiding on the roof, Meng Zheng saw clearly what they were doing. When the rooster crowed at around five o'clock in the morning, the rich man and his wife began to nap, so Meng Zheng came down from the roof by a rope, with a duck in his arms. He stood quietly behind them to wait for a chance. When the rich man wanted to give the rooster to his wife with his eyes closed, Meng Zheng hurriedly passed the duck to the woman and took the rooster away.

The woman held the duck for a while. Then she touched the duck's mouth with eyes closed and asked the rich man, "Why is the rooster's mouth flat?" The rich man was so sleepy that he also could not open his eyes and said with confidence, "Because it is going to crow."

When the rich man and his wife woke up and saw the duck in their arms, they knew that the rooster had been replaced by Meng Zheng again.

# 故事三十八　继母

　　从前有两兄妹,母亲早死,继母性情凶狠,常常虐待他们。一天,继母把谷撒到田埂上,然后在丈夫面前说:"他们只会吃饭,不会做工,叫他们到田里看禾,却到山上采野果吃,丢了不少谷子。"她又说:"他们喜欢上山,就让他们到深山谷里去采野果,自己生活好了,免得以后连累我们。"父亲信以为真,就带他们兄妹俩到远远的深山谷里去,而自己却一个人偷偷地回来了。

　　兄妹俩在山谷里找不到父亲,才知道是受骗了,两人互相抱着,大哭了一场。哭着哭着,竟在石头上睡着了。

　　第二天早上,他俩醒来,向四面望了一下,身边什么东西都没有,只有父亲留下的那把刀。这时,他们又渴又饿,到哪里找东西吃呢?没有办法,只好喝山沟里的水充饥。他们走到山沟里,看到一只死了的山鹿,高兴极了,便把山鹿割开来,割了一些鹿肉。可是,深谷里没有火,怎么办?到外面去找吧,不行,重重高山峻岭,要走好几天,而且又不识路。他们想来想去,看看地下,望望青天,想不出办法。这时,刚好有一只喜鹊飞来,停在他们旁边的树枝上。他们便哭着对喜鹊说道:"喜鹊!喜鹊!可怜我们小小的手、小小的脚,走不出深山,眼看要饿死了!喜鹊!喜鹊!请帮我们找把火,找个罐子和小碗吧!"

　　不一会,喜鹊带来了他们需要的东西。兄妹俩心里非常高兴,忙把鹿肉煮熟,饱餐一顿。可是,他们在高兴过后,又忧愁起来。他们想:日子长着呢,吃完了,以后日子怎么过呢?兄妹正在忧愁,忽然听见"噼噼啪啪"的声音,一只斑鸠飞来了,又停在那棵树枝上,叫着:"咕咕!自由!快活!不饥不饿,谷子、瓜子、菜子满肚。"哥哥听了忙拿起自制的弓箭一射,斑鸠被射落下来了。

他们连忙割开它的肚子,取出谷子、玉米、菜子、瓜子、豆子,拿它们做种子,开荒耕种了。

第二年,他们获得丰收,生活过得很好。他们种的瓜大得惊人,一个人抱也抱不过来,搬也搬不动;瓜蔓长得很长,从山谷延过高山,一直伸延到他们原来的家里。他们的恶母愚父看到这根瓜蔓觉得有点奇怪,就跟着瓜蔓一直走去,结果他们看到是自己的孩子,便羞得不敢抬头,心中又恨又恼。不过,既然见面了,他们只好装着哭脸说:"为了你俩,害得我们好苦呀!我们不知道穿过多少高山,越过多少深谷,跨过多少长江大河,才把你们找到啊!回去吧,家里总是比这里好得多啊!"可是,他们兄妹俩早已厌恶那个家庭,便说:"这里是最幸福的地方,因为它是我们劳动创造出来的。我们再也不想回家里去了。为了报答你们的'恩情',我们送给你们一个瓜壳,里面装有宝贵的东西。但是,你们要记住,路上千万别把它打开来,那会什么也得不到的。"于是继母拿了一个大的,父亲拿了一个小的,回家去了。

愚父恶母回到家里,各自掰开带回来的瓜壳,伸手进去,想拿宝贝。只见愚父伸手进去,连忙缩了回来,口里嚷着:"痛死人了!"恶母伸手进去,面即变色,站也站不住,倒地昏了过去。原来,愚父被瓜壳里的蜈蚣咬伤了,痛得死去活来;恶母给毒蛇咬了一口,毒气攻心,不久就死了。

## The Stepmother

Once upon a time there was a brother and a sister whose mother died early while their stepmother was fierce and often bullied them. One day, the stepmother sprinkled the grain on the ridge of the field and said to her husband, "They can only eat but could not work. When I told them to go to the fields to work, they went to the mountains to pick wild fruits. In the end, they lost a lot of millet." She added, "Since they like going up to the mountains, why not let them go to the deep valley to pick wild fruits and live on their own? Thus they will not bother us in the future."As a result, their father believed her, and took the brother and the sister far away into the deep valley, then he secretly came back alone.

The brother and the sister didn't know they had been cheated until they couldn't find their father in the valley. They hugged each other and cried loudly. Later they got tired and fell asleep on the stone.

The next morning when they woke up, they found nothing but the machete their father had left behind. They were thirsty and hungry, so they had no choice but to drink water from the gully. They went forward to the ravine and saw a dead wild deer. They were very happy and cut some pieces of venison. However, there was no fire and they couldn't cook the venison. They decided to go outside to look for fire. Unfortunately, the mountains were so high that they didn't know when they could go out. What's worse, they didn't know the way out. They thought about it over and over, looking down at the ground and up at the blue sky, but still could not think of a way. Just then, a magpie flew near and stopped on a branch of the tree next to them. They cried to the magpie, "Magpie! Magpie! Please take pity on our little hands and feet. We could not get out of the mountain, and we are going to starve to death! Magpie! Magpie! Please help us find a fire, a jar and a small bowl."

After a while, the magpie really brought what they needed. The brother and the sister were so happy that they quickly cooked the venison and had a good meal. But after that, they became sad again, as there was still a long way to go. They thought: After this meal, how can we make a living? The brother and the sister were worried about themselves when they heard the sound of crackling. A turtledove flew near and stopped on the branch. The turtledove cried, "Goo! Goo! Freedom! Happy! My belly is full of millet, melon seeds and vegetable seeds, and you'll not be hungry." Hearing these words, the brother hurriedly shot down the turtledove with his self-made bow and arrow. They hurriedly cut its belly open and took out the millet, corn, vegetable seeds, melon seeds, beans and began to cultivate the wasteland.

In the second year, they had a bumper harvest and began to live a good life. The melons they planted were too big to be hugged or moved, and the melon vines grew so long that it even stretched across the valleys and mountains to their original home. Their evil mother and foolish father felt a little strange when they saw the melon vines, so they followed them all the way to the valley. When they saw their children, they were ashamed, and felt very regretful and resentful. But now that they had met them, they pretended to cry for their misery. The mother said, "We worried about you so much after you got lost. We have crossed mountains, valleys and rivers before we found you. Let's go back home. Our home is much better than this place!" However, the brother and the sister had already hated their family, so they replied, "This is the happiest place, because we created it. We will never go back home. In order to repay your 'kindness', we give you each a melon shell containing precious things. But remember not to open it on the way, otherwise, you'll get nothing." And then the stepmother took a big one and the father took a small one home.

When the foolish father and the evil mother came home, they broke the melon shells to get something. The foolish father reached his hand in but drew back hurriedly, shouting, "It hurts!" The evil mother put her hand in, and her face immediately changed. Then she couldn't stand on her feet and got faint on the ground. It turned out that the foolish father was bitten by the centipede in the melon shell and the evil mother was bitten by a poisonous snake in the melon shell. As a result, the foolish father got badly hurt and the evil mother died soon.

## 故事三十九 藤桥救妹

在海南岛崖州东渡至万州（今万宁市）的半途中，有一条又深又宽的大河，叫作藤桥溪。它发源于五指山西麓的毛感、毛瑞尖岭，流经保亭营四弓、五弓、首弓、南山至崖州藤桥附近的陵水湾，注入南海。

相传，很早很早以前，溪东住着一个黎族青年，名叫阿洛。阿洛刚出世不久，父母便因饥寒交迫先后死去了。阿洛很会爬树，饿了，就爬上高入云天的大树，采摘黑莓、枇杷、野果吃。他很会射箭，逃奔的野猪、黄猄，他随手拈弓搭箭一放，就应声倒地。他很会捕鱼，弯身入水，用手一摸，蹦蹦跳跳的大鱼就被他捕上来。他很会吹箫，鸟儿听见了，都飞到他跟前，喜得在树上飞上飞下；云彩听见了，被迷住而忘却移步，停在半空，凝在山头；风儿听见了很高兴，快乐地把他那优美的箫声传遍周围，传到溪面，让大家一起享受。溪西住着一位黎族姑娘，被清脆优美的箫声迷住了。她站在溪边，一手扶着椰子树杆，一手搭着眼睫眉心，踮起脚跟，隔溪远眺，凭着箫声，寻踪觅迹。夜风吹来不觉凉，雨露湿透不觉冷。她胸中像是冒出了一股温泉，流布全身，暖烘烘、热乎乎的；心里似是灌满了蜜糖，甜丝丝的，又似喝了山兰糯米酒，醉迷迷的，仿佛天地间什么也不存在，只有那清脆婉转、优美动人的箫声。姑娘恨不得长出一双翅膀飞过溪去，伴着箫声，唱起山歌、跳起舞。

溪西这位姑娘名叫阿香，今年十六岁，比阿洛小两岁。她长得非常好看，生着一对弯弓新月似的蛾眉，一双水灵灵的凤眼，一张樱桃似的殷红小嘴，她轻轻一笑，两颊有醉人的笑窝。她跟她妈妈学会了织筒裙的好手艺，学会了一口胜似天籁的山歌，鸟儿听见了，都来到她跟前，喜得在树上飞上飞下，云彩听见了，也被迷住，忘却移步，凝在山头，停在半空。阿香长得人人喜爱，四面八方、远远近近的后生都来找她对歌求亲，她也热情地欢迎前来与求亲的后生对歌。

她唱道：

"有心求亲妹应允，

先唱支歌解心闷，

哥如若赢跟哥去，

妹如若输上哥门。"

众后生听了很高兴，纷纷上前唱起来。歌声一阵接一阵，一轮连一轮，从鸡啼唱到日头落，从月出唱到东边亮，一连唱了三天三夜，唱了三夜又三天，但是，都没有人唱赢她。

一传十，十传百，对歌求亲的消息立刻传到了溪东。溪东的阿洛听见了立刻赶来看热闹。后生们瞧见大名鼎鼎的歌手阿洛站在后边，只是笑，不开口，便推他出去和阿香对一对歌。阿洛的脸红了一阵又一阵，后来壮了壮胆子，就开腔和阿香对起歌来。后生们的喝彩声、掌声一阵热似一阵。他俩从鸡啼唱到日落，从月出唱到东边亮，一连唱了七天又七夜，唱了七夜又七天。最后，阿洛唱赢了，后生们都围拢过来祝贺他。阿香也解下绣花头帕送给他，当作定情订婚的信物。阿洛看见这信物，便慌了；心里好像钻进了一只兔子蹦蹦地跳，脸蛋好像喝了山兰酒一般红了一阵又一阵。阿香也脸蛋红扑扑地跟上前去，说："对歌之前我讲过：哥如若赢跟哥去，妹如若输上哥门。阿哥！溪水流去不流回，说话出口永难收！"阿洛是多么地喜欢阿香，走遍天涯海角，踏断大路小畦，也找不到第二个阿香。但是，他想起自己是个无依无靠、穷苦贫困的人，不忍心让阿香跟着受罪，便唱道：

"哥想讨亲无人嫁，

谁都弃嫌哥穷家，

人屋家大乜都有，

哥屋家穷吃薯芽。"

阿香立即答唱道：
"哥想讨亲妹就嫁，
妹不弃嫌哥穷家，
人屋家大妹不要，
妹愿心甜吃薯芽。"
阿洛又唱道：
"哥想讨亲无人肯，
谁都弃嫌哥单身，
人屋家大乜都有，
哥屋家穷吃薯藤。"
阿香立即答唱道：
"哥想讨亲妹就肯，
妹不弃嫌哥单身，
人屋家大妹不要，
妹愿心甜吃薯藤。"

于是，阿洛和阿香定了亲，定在农历八月十五结婚。姑娘们都日夜赶着绣花，要送给阿香当彩礼；后生们都去酿山兰糯米酒，要送给阿洛设宴席。

消息传到了有钱有势的蒂闷耳朵里。蒂闷气得双手发抖，双腿打战，脸上青盖紫，紫盖黑。他暴跳起来，声音在屋顶上滚；拍起桌子来，桌子破开了一个大窟窿；摔起凳子来，凳子就断了四条腿。他喊来管家斥问："叫你去下聘，要娶阿香当媳妇，不把人接回来，却嫁给了阿洛，是怎么一回事？"管家回答说："阿香讲，公子长得太漂亮了，她配不上。"原来，蒂闷的儿子跛脚拐手秃头顶，烂眼歪嘴凹牙槽，满身上下都生疮，流脓流血，又腥又臭，苍蝇、蚊子成群围着他转。他四处找，都找不着对象。蒂闷听说阿香长得好看，聪明伶俐，四方后生都看上她，当天就打发管家带着彩礼去求亲。不料，被阿香拒绝，顶了回来，还被对歌的后生们奚落了一场。管家对蒂闷说："先下手为强，后下手遭殃。"蒂闷就派了几十名家丁、打手，偷偷摸摸，连夜到阿香家，把阿香抢了过来，要阿香和他的儿子成亲。阿香又哭又闹，把家丁咬得满身青一块紫一块。阿香又悲愤又痛苦，哭得天昏地暗，死去活来，连苍天也可怜她的遭遇：雷公隆隆号叫，惊得天崩地裂；树木也在暴风雨中放声号哭，痛苦悲伤得前倾后倒；大溪痛苦得泪水滚滚，溪水一下子暴涨十丈，把两岸许多低洼的田野、村子都淹没了。

阿香被抢的消息传到了阿洛的耳朵里，阿洛如同吞了烧火棍，满胸怒火，痛苦欲绝。他立即拿起弓箭和钩刀，冲出去，要把阿香救出来。但是，水大连天，他过不了溪。这时，他已不顾自己的生命，即使自己千死万死，也要冲过去救阿香。当他正要纵身一跃跳下溪的时候，一只鹩哥飞来伏在他的肩头上，说："阿洛，阿洛，水大连天怎么能过得去，你淹死了，谁来救阿香？"阿洛问："鹩哥，鹩哥，你说得对，但是我能怎么办？救不出阿香，我怎么活？"鹩哥说："阿洛，阿洛，不要慌，在这条溪的尽头，有座尖岭，尖岭后的毛感山，有个大龙石洞，你去那里求求龙公公，只有他能帮你救阿香。"阿洛还要说什么，只见鹩哥已飞上云天去了。阿洛立即起身，按照鹩哥的指点，沿着溪岸，奔向毛感山大龙洞去。

阿洛越走山越高，越走涧越深。遇着高山大岭，他附着石壁一步一步向上爬；来到悬崖深涧，他抓住古树垂下的野藤一荡而过。手磨破了，他剥木棉树皮包扎好了又继续爬；脚长血泡了，他剥椰子树皮包裹了又继续走；风寒雨冷，又饿又累，他伏在溪边，喝水喝到饱，又继续奔走。从天黑走到日出，从日出走到天黑，一连走了三天三夜，他终于来到了溪的尽头。溪的尽头，果然有一座尖岭，他抬头看，山如同一把巨大的锥子，拔地而起，顶天而立，白云缭绕在半山腰。这时，他把手脚上的伤口包扎牢，又继续攀藤附葛，越过尖岭，来到巍峨挺拔的毛感山。

毛感山真的有一个巨大的石洞。阿洛放眼一看，洞里石凳成行，一条巨大的金龙盘身卧在宝座上，周身发亮，两眼发光。阿洛连忙上前，三跪九叩，顶礼膜拜，恳求龙公公大发慈悲救救阿香。

龙公公说:"勇敢的年轻人,我赐你一支宝藤,你骑上它,闭上眼睛,它能把你送到家。等到它说'好了',你才睁开眼。然后,把藤架在溪上,它能帮你过河救阿香。走吧,勇敢的年轻人!"阿洛听了又一连拜了几拜。抬头睁眼一看,龙公已不见了,只见石椅上放着一支长丈余的宝藤。他双手拿过宝藤,翻身骑上,闭着眼睛,感觉腾空而起,两耳生风,无翼而飞。仅半碗饭功夫,只听宝藤说:"好了!"阿洛睁开眼睛,果然已回到家的溪边。他拿起宝藤,在溪上一架,宝藤便变成一座又长又宽的藤桥,横架大溪西东。阿洛立刻冲过溪去,杀入蒂闷家的牢房,救出阿香和被关在一起的诸位黎族姐妹。蒂闷发现了,立刻带领家丁追赶。阿洛背着阿香,急急忙忙在前面跑,蒂闷带领家丁紧紧在后面追。阿洛背着阿香走上了藤桥,蒂闷和家丁也追上了藤桥。他们相隔只有一竿远,眼看就要抢着了。阿洛背着阿香刚一跑过藤桥,巨大的藤桥立刻复原,变成一条又短又小的藤。蒂闷和家丁纷纷坠入溪中,被洪水淹死了。阿洛和阿香双双上前,要把宝藤扶起,宝藤说:"有情人终成眷属!勇敢的年轻人,祝你们永远幸福!"阿洛和阿香双膝跪地,千恩万谢。当他们抬头起身时,宝藤已变成一条巨龙,朝着大溪头、毛感山大龙洞的方向腾空而去了。

从此,阿洛和阿香成了亲,早出晚归,你亲我爱,生活过得很美满。乡亲们也安居乐业,过着太平的日子。为了感谢龙公帮助阿洛救出阿香的恩情,人们便把这座仙藤称为藤桥,把这条溪称为藤桥溪。藤桥溪两岸椰林苍翠,山明水秀,风景秀丽,土地肥沃,物产富饶。这里居住着黎、汉两族同胞,海口至榆林的东线公路从这里横穿而过,后来是海南黎族苗族自治州崖县藤桥镇所在地。

# The Tengqiao[①]

On the way from Yazhou to Wanzhou (now Wanning City), there is a deep and wide river called Tengqiao River (ratten bridge river). It originates from the Maogan and Maorui Range of the western Wuzhishan Mountain, passes along several villages of Baoting County, and flows into the South China Sea through Lingshui Bay near the Tengqiao of Yazhou.

According to legend, a long time ago, there was a Li youth named Aluo living on the east bank of the river. When Aluo was very young, his parents died of poverty and left Aluo alone. Aluo was very good at climbing trees. When he was hungry, he could climb up big trees to pick blackberries, loquats and wild fruits to eat. He was good at archery and could shoot wild animals with his bow and arrows. He was good at fishing. As soon as he touched the big fish in deep water with his hands, he could catch it. He was good at playing the flute. Hearing the music he played with the flute, birds would came to him and flew up and down on the trees with joy, clouds would keep still on top of the mountains, and wind would be pleased to spread the beautiful music all around for everyone. There lived a Li girl on the west bank of the river who was fascinated by the beautiful music. She used to lean against a coconut tree by the river side with one hand raising on her eyelashes to listen to the music. She would tiptoe to trace the origin of the music far across the river, without caring about the cold night wind or the wet rain. Her heart felt sweet like being filled with honey, and she seemed to be drunk with Shanlan glutinous rice wine. The girl wanted to grow a pair of wings to fly across the river, singing folk songs and dancing with the music.

---

① Rattan Bridge.

The girl was named Axiang, who was 16 years old, two years younger than Aluo. Axiang was very good-looking, with a pair of crescent-like eyebrows, bright and watery eyes, cherry-like mouth and rosy cheeks with dimples. She learned the skill of weaving skirts from her mother and was skilled in it. She sang folk songs which were even more fascinating than heavenly music. When birds heard her singing, they all came to her and flew up and down on the tree with joy. When clouds heard her singing, they were also fascinated and forgot to move from mountains. Everyone liked Axiang. Young men from near and far came to sing antiphonal songs to win her heart and Axiang warmly welcomed them.

She sang the following song,

"I will agree with your request,

But let's sing a song first.

If you beat me in singing,

I'll go beat you home."

All the young men were very happy and went forward to sing one after another. They sang for three days and nights, but no one beat her.

The news spread from person to person and soon it spread to the east bank of the river. When Aluo heard this, he immediately came to the west bank of the river to see the fun. As soon as the other young people saw Aluo, the famous singer, standing behind silently and smiling, they pushed him out and asked him to sing antiphonal songs with Axiang. Aluo blushed for a while and then began to sing with Axiang. The songs they sang were so charming that they got waves of cheers and applause from the crowd. They sang for seven days and nights from sunrise to sunset, from evening to morning. Finally, Aluo won. All the young people gathered around to congratulate him. Axiang gave her embroidered handkerchief to Aluo as a token of affection and engagement. Aluo was so excited and embarrassed that his heart thumped hard and his face flushed like drunk with Shanlan rice wine. Axiang went forward shyly and said to Aluo, "I have promised that I will marry the man who defeats me in singing. My words are like the river flowing forward, which can not be taken back." Of course Aluo loved Axiang and wanted to marry her. But considering his poor condition, he was afraid that he couldn't promise Axiang a good life, so he answered with the following song,

"No girl wants to marry me,

Because of my poor family.

Others may have big houses;

I only live on sweet potato sprouts."

Axiang immediately replied with a song,

"If you want to marry me,

I won't mind your poor condition.

I don't care about big house,

but like sweet potato sprouts."

Hearing this, Aluo sang again,

"No girl wants to marry me,

As I am living on my own.

Others may have big houses,

I only live on sweet potato vines."

Axiang immediately replied with another song,

"You can marry me if your want,

I don't mind if you are alone.

I don't care other's big house,

I'd eat sweet potato vine with you."

So Aluo and Axiang were engaged and decided to marry on August 15th of lunar calendar. In order to give Axiang a bride's gift, the young girls were busy with embroidery day and night; in order to help Aluo prepare for a wedding banquet, the young boys went to brew Shanlan glutinous rice wine.

The news reached the ears of the rich and powerful man named Dimen. Dimen's face was red with anger and his limbs began to tremble. He sprang up, overthrew the table and stools, and roared to the housekeeper, "I let you make Axiang marry my son, but why is she going to marry Aluo? What's wrong?" The housekeeper replied, "Axiang says that the young master is too beautiful for her." It turned out that Dimen's son was lame and bald, with rotten eyes, crooked mouth and concave teeth. His body which was covered with sores and pus was so smelly that flies and mosquitoes swarmed around him. He tried hard but could find no girl willing to marry him. When Dimen heard that Axiang was beautiful and smart, he sent the housekeeper with betrothal gifts to make a proposal. Unexpectedly, the housekeeper was rejected by Axiang and ridiculed by the young men singing antiphonal songs. The housekeeper suggested to Dimen, "It's better to snatch her immediately than to wait until you get nothing." So Dimen sent dozens of servants and thugs to Axiang's house that night, and snatched Axiang to marry his son. Axiang cried loudly and bit those who came near her. Axiang cried so sadly that even heaven pitied her. Leigong roared loudly to tear the earth apart; the trees howled sadly in the storm; the river burst into tears so the river water reached to a high level, drowning many low-lying fields and villages.

The news of Axiang's being snatched reached Aluo's ears. Aluo was so angry and sad, and his chest was like being filled with burning fire. He immediately picked up the bow and arrows and sword, rushed out to save Axiang. However, the river was too deep and broad for him to get across. Aluo had already disregarded his own safety, and he would die to save Axiang. When he was about to jump into the river, a bird fell on his shoulder and cried, "Aluo, Aluo, how can you cross the deep water in this way? If you were drowned, who will save Axiang?" Aluo asked, "Bird, bird, you're right, but what else can I do? How can I live if I can't save Axiang?" The bird replied, "Aluo, Aluo, don't worry. At the end of the river, there is a sharp ridge. Behind the sharp ridge there is a big cave in the Maogan Mountain, where Longgong (Master Dragon) lives. Go there and ask Longgong for help. Only he can help you save Axiang." With these words, the bird flew away. Aluo got off immediately to the Maogan Mountain along the river bank to find Longgong according to the bird's instruction.

The mountains were higher and higher, and the rivers were deeper and deeper, but Aluo kept moving on without a stop. When he met the high peaks, he attached himself to the rock wall and climbed up step by step; when he came to the cliff and deep river, he grabbed the wild vines hanging from the old trees and swung past; when his hands were worn out, he bound them with kapok bark; when his feet were blistered, he wrapped them with coconut peel; when he was hungry and tired, he bent down by the river and drank water. After three days and nights, he finally came to the end of the river and got to the sharp ridge. He looked up and saw that the mountain stood upright against the sky like a huge awl, with white clouds winding around the mountainsides. He bandaged up the wounds on his hands and feet, and continued to climb the mountain via the vines. In the end, he reached the splendid Maogan Mountain.

There was a huge cave in the Maogan Mountain. In the cave lined up stone benches, and a huge golden Chinese dragon whose whole body was bright and eyes were shining was lying on the throne. Aluo quickly came forward, knelt down and kowtowed. He begged Longgong to be merciful and save Axiang. Longgong said, "Brave young man, I give you a precious rattan. Riding on it with your eyes closed, it will take you home. Wait until it says 'All right.' before opening your eyes. Then, put the rattan on the river, it can help you cross the river to save Axiang. Go ahead, brave young man." Aluo bowed several times to thank Longgong. But when he looked up, he found the dragon disappeared, leaving a precious long rattan on the stone throne. He took the precious rattan in both hands and rode on it. With his eyes closed, he felt like he was flying up in the air and his ears were full of the sound of wind. Before long, he heard the precious rattan said "All right.", so Aluo opened his eyes and found that he had returned to the river near his home. He picked up the precious rattan and put it on the river. The rattan immediately became a long and wide bridge across the river. Aluo rushed across the river and ran into Dimen's house. He rescued Axiang and other Li girls who were imprisoned together. As soon as Dimen found out, he ordered the servants to catch Aluo. Aluo carried Axiang on his back and ran forward in a hurry. Dimen led his servants to chase him closely behind. When Aluo carried Axiang on his back and got on the rattan bridge, Dimen and his servants also got on the rattan bridge. They were about to be snatched. As soon as Aluo ran over the bridge with Axiang on his back, the huge bridge immediately turned into a short and small rattan. Dimen and his servants fell into the river and were drowned by the flood. Aluo and Axiang came forward to lift the rattan up. The rattan said, "The lovers will get married at last! Brave young couple, I wish you happiness forever!" Aluo and Axiang knelt down on their knees and thanked the rattan. When they stood up, they found the precious rattan had turned into a giant dragon, flying away in the direction of the Maogan Mountain.

After that, Aluo and Axiang got married. They worked very

diligently every day. They loved each other and lived a happy life. The villagers also lived and worked in peace. In order to thank Longgong, people named the rattan Tengqiao and the river Tengqiao River. On both sides of the river, there are green coconut forests, beautiful mountains and rivers. The land is fertile with rich products. The eastern line expressway from Haikou to Yulin passes through this place where lives the Li and Han people. Now it is the site of Tengqiao Town in Yazhou District of Hainan Li and Miao Autonomous Prefecture.

## 故事四十　老课将军

很久很久以前，古老的海南岛上，在五指山西麓的南圣河畔，八面山下，有一个番峨村。村里有位黎族青年，因为他善于撒谎，远近闻名，人们便给他起了一个外号叫作"老课"①。叫着叫着，日长年久，叫上口了，人们却把他的名字忘掉了。

老课长着一副竖眉鱼眼，偏嘴尖鼻，高额骨，长下巴。他从小任性，调皮淘气，说的谎如同南圣河里的石头一样大，千层牛皮也吹得破。每天，他去放牛，都上山爬树，掏鸟窝，捉鸟儿。他还会用波罗蜜果的黏液涂在竹篾片上，在竹篾片的下端系着一块石头和一只小蟋蟀，将其插在山旁沟坎，缚在树枝、架子上，鸟儿看见了蟋蟀，便飞来吃，有时更是几只成群齐飞来，你争我夺，互相抢吃。鸟儿在扑腾时碰着竹篾上的黏液，被黏液粘住了翅膀和羽毛，便飞不走了。每天，他都能捉很多很多鸟。他捉到了鸟，便在鸟的屁股处串上一支竹箭，拿到村里，在青年伙伴面前，到处夸耀吹嘘，说这些鸟都是他用箭射下来的，并且每只都是射中屁股。一传十，十传百，远近的人们都满口夸赞老课箭法好，本领高，日后必定娶得一个最漂亮的姑娘，当一个八面威风的常胜将军。老课听了众人的夸赞，喜得眉在额角上飞，目在皮缝里笑，嘴巴扒到耳根下，耳朵吊到肩头上，鼻尖朝着天顶，双手捧着肚腹哈哈大笑，仿佛现在他就是一员常胜将军，身边有位年轻漂亮的妻子陪伴着，好不威风。

老课箭法如神的消息传到了八面山峒主的耳朵里。峒主叫来管家探问，证实了果然有此奇迹，他高兴极了。原来，八面山有一只

---

①　黎语"骗子"。

山猪精，时常四处伤人，不久前，八面山峒主的儿子进山去找姑娘幽会，归来时，在八面山上被凶恶的山猪精咬死了，峒主一家哭得死去活来。时到今日，他们还是悲痛欲绝，恨不得有朝一日捉住山猪精来剥皮，切成碎块，放盐来腌。此时，峒主听说老课箭法高强，喜出望外。峒主立刻吩咐管家，带上家丁，抬着大轿，把老课请到家里来，设宴款待。老课眼睛滴溜溜地打转，伶俐乖巧，知道赴宴饮酒与箭有关，于是，不忘佩弓带箭，精心装束打扮，也显得添了几分勇士色彩。席上摆满又肥又嫩的白切鸡，又烂又香的炖猪腿、羊肉，还有山珍海味，各款各式，花样繁多，峒主还挖出埋在芭蕉丛下的陈年糯米酒，亲自把壶款待老课。

酒过数巡，峒主热情洋溢地说："年轻人，你射鸟箭法如神，堪称旷古未闻，空前绝后！"老课听了，醉上加醉，心里甜丝丝、热乎乎的。接着，峒主又说："如此高强的本领，要为保山护民做出贡献，才称得上英雄豪杰。此间八面山上，有一山猪精，神出鬼没，常常伤人。你若能捉获山猪精，我愿赏铜锣①百口，牛羊百只，田地百亩，甜酒百缸，并愿以小女的终身相托！"

老课起初听说叫他去捉山猪精，吓得酒醒大半，魂不附体，满头大汗。后来听说重重有赏，还能娶峒主的亲生闺女做老婆，便乐如神仙，得意扬扬。他见利眼红，色胆包天，"嘭"的一声站立起来，干了一碗酒，抹了一下口，便声高气壮地说："好！不要说一只山猪精，就是千只百只，也如瓮中捉鳖，手到擒来，不在话下。"峒主亲手把壶，又敬了他一碗。老课也不谦让，一饮而尽，浑身是胆地说："古往今来，大凡勇士都是说行就走，不行就止，我现在就去，诸位请了！"老课摸摸弓箭，觉得这并不是自己的拿手锐器，正好墙角有把钩刀，他急中生智，装作箭落弯身拾箭，偷偷地顺手拿过钩刀，藏在身侧，遮遮掩掩地出门而去。

老课独自一人来到八面山上。刚才因贪饮了几碗，此时他酒兴

---

① 黎族人民过去没有货币，只能拿货物交换，一个铜锣相当于十头牛。

# 第五章
## 黎族经典民间故事汉英对照

大作,醉醺醺的,一脚高,一脚低,边走边想。他那一双醉眼,只见峒主双手给他献上口口铜锣,缸缸甜酒,群群牛羊,又见峒主的闺女笑眯眯地向他走来,给他敬酒。他心中好像灌满了蜜糖,又甜又乐。

这时,一阵山风骤起,一只肥大如牛的山猪精,嘴角两边一对弯牙向上翘,好像举着两把锐利的尖刀,连跳带滚凶猛地向他扑来。从古以来,谁也没见过这么凶猛的大怪物。老课一看,吓得酒意大醒,魂飞魄散,急忙转身,拔脚就跑,连呼:"救命!救命!"老课慌不择路,好高好高的棘丛他都纵身一跃,翻飞而过。山猪精紧紧地追,老课拼命地落荒而逃,仅有数步之近,眼看就要追上了。前面不远,横着悬崖绝壁,百丈深渊,迫在眉睫,危在旦夕。老课看见崖畔路旁刚好有一株大榕树,枝叶参天,树干粗壮。他急中生智,绕着大榕树转。山猪精善于直冲,笨于转弯。山猪精冲到树前,他纵身一跃,走到树后。双方互相周旋。山猪成精,也有一智,它瞧见大榕树的气根凭空下垂,落地成木,根干难分,好像大榕树有着数条粗大的树干,紧挨相连,中间夹缝可以过身,便从树干、树根的夹缝之间瞄准老课,凶猛直冲。不料,树间夹缝稍狭,山猪精冲过半身,便被拦腰夹住。冲不过,退不得,嗷嗷吼叫,如雷贯耳,震得山谷轰鸣,地动山摇。老课上前,挥舞钩刀,用刀背对准山猪精脑袋狠狠猛打,山猪精挣扎着惨叫一声,头歪脚直,不动了。

他抓住山猪精,用力猛拉,拉不出,便用钩刀把榕树根砍断,山猪精翻倒一旁,四脚朝天。他又拿出一支竹箭,对准山猪精屁股插进去。他用了九牛二虎之力,要把山猪精背回去报功请赏,但背不动。他便连忙回村,报告峒主。峒主派了七八个粗壮男丁,执棒拿绳去扛回来。峒主和众人看见利箭不偏不倚,正好射中山猪精的屁股,都夸赞老课箭法如神,说他孤身上山,杀死山猪精,为民除了一害,真是英雄虎胆,本领超群,智勇非凡。峒主依其诺言,立刻唤来八音乐手,奏乐吹打,热烈庆贺;拿出铜锣、牛群,缠上锦帕，献给老课；吩咐婢女布置洞房，引出闺女，和老课当夜成亲。八面山的乡亲邻里都来祝贺，好不热闹。

　　从此，老课的名声越来越大，一直传到了官府老爷的耳朵里。不久以前，一群海盗常常从海上窜到海南岛深山黎寨，抢劫财物，掳掠妇女，无恶不作。海盗人多势众，连官军也敌不过他们，从别地调兵救援，又远水救不了近火，官府老爷正在为此而日夜愁闷。这时，官府老爷听说八面山黎峒出了个单身除妖、箭法如神的勇士老课，便发下委任状，委任老课为将军，拨兵一千，前往剿除海盗。

　　老课在峒主家成亲，日日开怀畅饮，夜夜欢歌乐舞。这天，突然门外传来说官府来人，要他领兵去剿除海盗。老课一听，有如五雷轰顶，吓蒙了，过了好大半天才神状稍定。老课想：这回死啦，死啦！这群海盗，官军都打不过他们，要自己带兵去征剿，这不是鸡仔赶老鹰，白白送死吗！打海盗，并非捉山猪精，捉鸟仔呵！想着想着，又情不自禁地叫出声来："死啦死啦，天哪！"他看了一眼官府来人，心脏扑通乱跳，脸上青里透白，白里透青，全无人色。一家人慌作一团，心急如焚，不知如何是好。

　　峒主坐在一角，一口一口地抽着生烟，满屋烟熏雾腾。他想：这群海盗，贼心野性，实在吓人惊众。但若不除，一旦窜到八面山来，不说其他乡邻，自己也自身难保。他"哎呀哎呀"地叹了几声，又壮起胆子，语无伦次地说："去也死，不去也死，还不如一试！女婿，你的箭射得那么准，山猪精那么凶也射死了，还害怕什么海盗不海盗！虽然海盗人多势众，但他们也是父母生的，有血有肉，或许不少也是贪生怕死的呢。"峒主一席杂杂乱乱的话，说得老课乱乱杂杂的心情柔顺了一半。他想着当将军的雄心宏愿，那个包天色胆又膨胀了起来。他说道："岳父说得有理，就这么办。"然后，他半悲半喜、患得患失地点兵磨箭，准备出征去了。

　　那群海盗劫掠了平原汉区、山村黎峒之后，正沿着南圣河，向八面山长驱直入。忽然，前哨探子回报："大王，不好了，小子探知，前面八面山黎峒有个大名鼎鼎的神箭手，名叫老课，他的箭法非常厉害，飞天老鹰，走土兔子，甚至蹦蹦跳跳的小麻雀，他都百发百中，并且个个都是射着屁股。前些天，在八面山上，也是他独自一人，深入险地，一箭射穿山猪精的屁股，把那常出没伤人的山猪精给杀了，八面峒主奖赏了他很多很多金银财物、珍珠宝贝，还把漂亮的闺女嫁了给他。官府老爷知道了，委他当讨海盗将军，统率千军万马，磨了满山的利箭，专门等着大王去哩！"

海盗大王厉声斥责道："废话，都是饭桶，快滚！"探子刚滚出门，他立即召来八大金刚、十大罗汉，聚集帐下商议。海盗大王帐下，金刚、罗汉站立躺卧，三五成群，你争我议，谁都说不服谁，拍得石板砰砰响，乱作一团。后来，还是一员坐在一旁低头捋须的金刚出谋献策说："兄弟们不要听探子说的那些灭了自己威风、长了别人志气的蠢话，吓唬得没了主见。我们此行，从茫茫大海到陆地深山，哪里不是一帆风顺，不攻而破，手到擒来，随心顺意！如今，就是千个老课，百个老课，又怎么样？他的弓箭只会专射屁股，那么我们每人都用一块铁板，挂在腰间，遮着屁股，不就赢了他了！"诸位金刚、罗汉都不约而同地竖起大拇指，称赞他："老兄高见，高见！"另一金刚说："等到攻破八面山，抢来姑娘，大小兄弟，每人都分一个，捉着那峒主的闺女、老课的新娘子，便献给大王做压寨夫人！"大家说的正中海盗大王下怀，只见他捧着肚腹"哈哈哈，哈哈哈"地笑得前仰后合。帐前帐后，迸发出一片"哈哈哈，哈哈哈"的狂笑声。

八面山上，团团埋伏着老课将军的官兵士卒。老课将军躲在石洞里。洞口挨近山头，居高临下，视野开阔，一览无余。因海盗人多势众，这场争斗凶吉未卜，只见老课双眼发愣，手抖脚颤。一位哨兵飞步翻身进洞传报："海盗来了！"老课一听，惊得满头大汗。他扶着石壁站起，扫视一番。只见海盗大王坐着踏脚竹轿，率领八大金刚、十大罗汉、数百大小喽啰，醉态朦胧，左摇右晃，黑压压地向八面山围袭而来。官军士卒都焦急地看着老课，看他有何计策。但是，老课已经惊得面色如土，六神无主，目瞪口呆了。眼看海盗已经窜到近前，官军士卒才迫不及待地叫唤："将军还不打呀？"老课一听，才如梦初醒，连呼："呃？快快打，打呀！"这时，号兵"呼呼呼"地吹响牛角，八面山的山头上，到处竖起"老课将军"的帅旗，战鼓响声震天动地，"冲呀，冲呀"的杀声四起，刀光闪闪，乱箭纷飞。

海盗不料老课将军就在眼前，不及提防。一望八面山的各个山头，到处都是"老课将军"帅旗，杀声如雷，箭如雨下，便个个吓得惊魂丧胆，晕头转向，拔腿就跑。因为跨的步子大，跑得飞快，两只脚踵都倒踢到挂在屁股上的那块铁板上，发出乒乒乓乓的声响。海盗们以为这都是老课将军的神箭射着屁股，更是好像乱了窝的排蜂，争先恐后，拼死逃命，自相践踏，死伤大半。其余的也喊爹叫娘，慌不择路，一口气跑到海边，争先登船，掉入海中，丧身鱼腹了。

海盗全军覆没了，众人才转身回望老课将军，不料老课将军也已惊得心慌至极，昏死在地了。老课将军的新娘子闻讯赶来，伏在他身上，又捏又捶，哭得死去活来。峒主也害怕老课将军一命归天，失去遮阴大树，于是，发出重赏，叫人抢救。诸位官兵拿来生姜、柚叶，擦鼻的擦鼻，松筋的松筋，折腾了大半天，老课将军才苏醒复活过来。他望见周围密密麻麻地站满许多人，以为都是海盗，又惊得缩作一团，口中连叫着："哎呀……"

# The General Laoke[①]

A long time ago, there was a village named Fan'e by the Nansheng River at the foot of the Bamian Mountain which belonged to the west range of the Wuzhishan Mountain on ancient Hainan Island. There was a

---

① The Liar.

Li youth in the village who was famous for his lying skills. People nicknamed him "Laoke", meaning "the liar" in the Li dialect. As time went by, people used to call his nickname and forgot his real name.

Laoke had a pair of vertical eyebrows, fish-like eyes, a pointed nose, a high forehead and a long chin. He was self-willed and mischievous from childhood. He liked to brag and his words were as unreal as the foams in the Nansheng River. Every day, when he went to herd cattle, he went up the mountain to climb trees, dig out bird nests and catch birds. He would also daub the jackfruit mucilage on bamboo strips, tie a stone and a small cricket at the bottom of each bamboo strip and put them in the ditches or on the branches and shelves. When the birds saw the crickets, they would fly near to eat them. Sometimes several birds flew together, competing for grabbing and eating the cricket, then their wings would flap on the mucus daubed on the bamboo strips and they got stuck. In this way, Laoke caught a lot of birds every day. Every time he caught the birds, he strung a bamboo arrow at the buttock of each bird and took the them back to the village. Then he boasted to his young peers that these birds were all shot down by him with arrows, and each one was shot in its buttock. People from far and near praised Laoke for his high skill in archery and said that he would marry the most beautiful girl and become an ever victorious general. Hearing such praises, Laoke laughed so loudly and happily that even his face was distorted. It seemed that he had become a victorious general, accompanied by a beautiful young wife.

The news that Laoke was highly skilled in archery reached the head of the Bamian Village. The head inquired the housekeeper about the news and got confirmed. The head was very happy. It turned out that there was a ferocious boar on the Bamian Mountain which often hurt people around. Not long ago, the son of the head was killed by the boar on his way back home from the mountain where he had had a tryst with a girl. The head's families were extremely grieved and the head wanted to have the boar killed to avenge his son's death. As soon as he heard that Laoke was highly skilled in archery, he was overjoyed. He immediately ordered the housekeeper to invite Laoke to his house by carrying him on a big sedan chair. Laoke was very clever. He knew that the invitation must have something to do with the arrows. Therefore, he did not forget to take his bow and arrows with him and dressed up carefully, which made him a little more like a worrier. The dining table was full of delicious food, including white cut chicken, stewed pig legs, mutton, and other delicacies. There were various kinds of dishes and the head even provided the precious glutinous rice wine which had been preserved for many years. The head entertained Laoke with wine and dine.

After several rounds of wine, the head said enthusiastically, "Young man, your skill of shooting birds is as good as the god, which I have never heard or seen." Hearing such praise, Laoke was so pleased, and felt even more drunk. Then, the head said again, "With such a high skill, you are supposed to make contributions to protect the mountain and the people, then you can be called a hero. In the Bamian Mountain, there is a fierce boar which often haunts around and hurts people. If you can catch it, I'd like to reward you with 100 gongs①, 100 cattle and sheep, 100 acres of land, 100 jars of sweet wine, and let my daughter marry you!"

At first, when Laoke heard that he was asked to catch the boar, he was so scared that he woke up from the drunkenness, sweating heavily. But later when he heard that there was a lot of rewards, and he could marry the daughter of the head, he became extremely happy and regained

---

① 1 gong equals to 100 cattle at that time.

courage again. He stood up excitedly, drank up a bowl of wine, wiped his mouth, and said in high voice, "All right! A fierce boar is nothing. I can catch hundreds of them easily. Catching boar to me is just like catching a turtle in a jar." The head took the wine pot to offer him another bowl of wine and toasted him. Laoke drank it all in one gulp and said boldly, "Since the ancient time, all the brave men would do what they had promised right away. I'll set out now. Goodbye!" With these words, Laoke touched his bow and arrows and thought that they were not good enough as weapon. He saw a hook knife hanging in the corner, so he pretended to bent over to pick up his arrow for secretly taking the hook knife. He hid it by his side, and went out.

Laoke came to the Bamian Mountain alone. He had drunk a few bowls of wine and his mind was not clear, so he staggered forward with one foot high and the other low. He daydreamed that the head was offering him gongs, jars of sweet wine, and flocks of cattle and sheep. He also saw through his drunken eyes the daughter of the head coming to offer him a toast. His heart seemed to be filled with honey, sweets and joy.

At that moment, with a gust of mountain wind, a strong mountain boar with a pair of curved teeth on both sides of its mouth turned upward. It seemed that it was holding two sharp knives, jumping and rolling fiercely towards him. No one had seen such a fierce monster. When Laoke saw it, he was so scared that he woke up from drunkenness and turned around to ran away, shouting for help loudly! In panic, Laoke jumped over the thorn bushes and run desperately, but the boar chased him closely. It was about to catch up with him and there was a cliff in front of him, so Laoke was in danger. Suddenly he saw a big banyan tree aside, with towering branches and strong stems. Laoke was quick-witted and ran around the big banyan tree. The boar was good at going straight but bad at turning around. When the boar rushed to the tree, Laoke turned around and ran to the back of the tree. The boar also had a sense of wisdom. When it saw the gap between the roots of the banyan tree, it rushed to the middle of the gap and wanted to pass through it. Unexpectedly, the gap between the roots was too narrow, and the boar was stuck between the air roots. The boar could not get out and roared like thunder, making the earth shaking. Seeing that his chance had come, Laoke waved the hook knife and hit the head of the boar with the back of the knife repeatedly. The boar was killed.

Laoke grabbed the boar and yanked it hard but couldn't pull it out, so he cut off the banyan roots with the hook knife. The boar fell over to the ground with four feet upward. Laoke took a bamboo arrow and thrust it into the ass of the boar. He tried hard to carry the boar back for reward, but he couldn't move it. He hastened back to the village and reported to the head who sent several stout men to carry it back with sticks and ropes. Seeing that the sharp arrow was just in the middle of the boar's ass, the head and other people all praised Laoke for his good skill of archery. They said that he went up the mountain alone and killed the boar, so he was a hero with courage, capability and extraordinary wisdom. According to the former promise, the head immediately called eight musicians to play music and celebrate it. He had his gongs and cattle wrapped with brocade handkerchiefs and presented them to Laoke. He also ordered his maidservants to decorate the bridal chamber and led her daughter to marry Laoke that night. In the Bamian Village, all the relatives and neighbors came to congratulate him.

Since then, Laoke's reputation had become higher and higher, which spread to the local governor's ears. It happened that a group of pirates often fled from the sea to the deep mountains of Hainan Island, robbing the villagers for property and women. Since the pirates were large in number and strong in weapon, the local governors couldn't win them and the soldiers from other places were too far to come for help. When the governor heard that a hero named Laoke in the Li village of the Bamian Mountain was good at killing boar demon by using bow and arrows, he issued a letter of appointment and appointed Laoke as a general, sending him 1000 soldiers to eliminate the pirates.

After Laoke got married in the head's home, he dined and wined every day, and sang and danced every night happily. One day news suddenly came that the governor wanted him to lead the troops to eliminate the pirates. Hearing that, Laoke was scared to death and couldn't come to himself for a long time. Laoke thought, "This time I will be done! Even the officials and soldiers are unable to win this group of pirates, how can I defeat them? Leading this troops to fight against the pirates is like using the chicken to drive the eagle. We'll die in vain! Besides, fighting against pirates is not like catching boars or birds!" Thinking about this, he could not help crying out, "I'm done! I'm done!" Looking at the messenger from the government, his heart was beating faster and faster and his face changed color with fear. The whole family was in a state of panic and anxiety, and they didn't know what to do.

The head sat in a corner smoking heavily, and the room was full of smoke. He thought that these pirates were really barbarous. If they were not eliminated, once they came to the Bamian Village, both his family and the villagers couldn't protect themselves. So he sighed a few times and said incoherently, "No matter you fight the pirates or not, you will die, so why not have a try? Your archery skill is so high that you even killed the boar with it, so you shouldn't be afraid of the pirates. Those pirates, though very fierce, are human beings and born of their parents. Maybe most of them are also greedy for life and afraid of death." Hearing these words, Laoke felt a little calm and comfortable. What's more, he was ambitious of becoming a general, so he said boldly, "You are right, my father-in-law. I'll do it." Then, with a confused feeling of half sadness and half happiness, he ordered his troops to sharpen the arrows and prepared to go to battle.

The pirates, after plundering the plain area where the Han people lived and the Li villages in the mountain area, were striding forward to the Bamian Mountain along the Nansheng River. All of a sudden, the sentinel reported, "My Chief, here comes the bad news. There is a famous archer named Laoke in the Li village of the Bamian Mountain. His archery skill is very high. He can shoot the flying eagles, the running rabbits, and even the jumping sparrows at the bottom. A few days ago, he went deep into the Bamian Mountain and shot the boar in its ass with an arrow. Since the boar had hurt many people, the head of the Bamian Village rewarded him with a lot of treasures, and married his beautiful daughter to him. And when the governor of the county knew this, he appointed Laoke as the general leading thousands of troops to fight against us. Now he has sharpened plenty of arrows and is waiting for us on the mountain!"

Hearing the sentinel's report, the pirate chief scolded him sternly, "Nonsense! You idiot! Get out of here quickly!" As soon as the sentinel got out of the barrack, the chief immediately summoned his counselors to discuss what to do next. The counselors standing or lying in the tent, discussed and quarreled with each other in different groups, some were suggesting doing this while others were suggesting doing that, all in a mess. Later, one counselor stroked his beard and gave such advice, "Brothers, don't believe the sentinel's stupid words and destroy your prestige. We have travelled from the vast sea to the land and mountains, and have done all the attacks without any difficulty. Even if there are thousands of persons like Laoke, we shouldn't be afraid of them. His bow and arrows can only shoot the buttocks, so why not hang an iron plate on our waist to cover our buttocks? In this way, we can defeat him easily!" All the other counselors and pirates unanimously agreed with his idea and praised him, "You've got a great idea!" Another counselor also said, "When the Bamian Mountain is conquered, we will snatch all the girls in the village and share them. The daughter of the head, the bride of Laoke will be offered to our chief as his wife." All the big talks met the needs of the pirate chief, so he held his belly and guffawed. The others all guffawed with him.

On the Bamian Mountain, officials and soldiers of General Laoke laid in ambush on the mountain. General Laoke was hiding in a cave with an entrance which was close to the top of the mountain in which they could take a broad view. As the pirates were powerful, the battle was uncertain. Laoke was horrified, with his eyes dazed and his limbs tremble. A sentry ducked into the cave and reported that the pirates were coming. Laoke startled to sweat. He stood up against the stone wall and looked outside. He saw that the chief of the pirates was sitting in a bamboo sedan chair, leading his counselors and hundreds of soldiers, marching towards the Bamian Mountain. The officials and soldiers looked anxiously at Laoke and waited for his order. However, Laoke was too horrified to think clearly. As the pirates were coming closer, the officials and soldiers couldn't wait to ask Laoke why not fight. As soon as Laoke heard these words, he woke up and ordered loudly, "Fight! Fight! Fight!" At this time, the bugler blew the horn, and the flags with the sign "General Laoke" were set up everywhere on top of the mountain. The war drums were beaten as loudly as the earth shaking; the sounds of "Rush! Rush!" were everywhere; the swords were shining and the arrows were flying in the air.

The pirates hadn't expected that General Laoke was in front of them. Seeing that the flags with the sign "General Laoke" were flying everywhere on the top of the mountain, the sound of soldiers were like thunder and the arrows were raining, all the pirates were scared to death. They turned around in a daze and began to run away. As they run quickly with long steps, both of their heels kicked the iron plate hanging on their buttocks, which rattled loudly. The pirates thought that they were shot by the arrows of General Laoke at their buttocks, and they were all in a mess. They scrambled to fight for their lives, trampled on each other and half of them were dead. The rest of the pirates ran to the seaside in a hurry and fell into the sea.

When the pirates were eliminated, all the soldiers turned to look at General Laoke who was unexpectedly frightened and fell into unconsciousness. General Laoke's bride came and fell on his body, pinching, thumping, and crying. The head was also afraid that General Laoke would die and they would lose the patron, so he issued a generous reward to save Laoke's life. Some officials and soldiers took ginger and pomelo leaves to rub Laoke's nose, and others massaged him. After a long time, General Laoke came back to life. As soon as he saw so many people standing around him, he mistook them as the pirates and rolled himself into a ball, crying "Oh!"

# 参考文献

[1] 保亭县文化馆. 黎族民间故事选：第一集［M］. 保亭：海南黎族苗族自治州人民印刷厂，1982.

[2] 陈超海，钟淑杯，邓小康. 黎族民间爱情悲剧文学审美论［J］. 文学教育（上），2015（4）.

[3] 陈兰. 试论黎族谚语［J］. 琼州学院学报，2012（4）.

[4] 陈立浩. 黎族文学试论［J］. 琼州学院学报，2007（4）.

[5] 陈立浩. 海南民族文学试论［J］. 海南师院学报，1993（1）.

[6] 陈立浩，范高庆，苏鹏程. 黎族文学概览［M］. 海口：海南出版社，2008.

[7] 董晓萍. 翻译与跨文化：解读（德）艾伯华《中国民间故事类型》的翻译经过、发现与意义：下［J］. 西北民族研究，2016（3）.

[8] 杜桐. 关于民间文学的加工创作问题：黎族叙事诗"甘工鸟"后记［J］. 理论与实践，1960（1）.

[9] 杜伟，杨雪. 论黎族民间童话的类型与特点［J］. 广东广播电视大学学报，2007（5）.

[10] 符桂花. 黎族民间故事大集［M］. 海口：海南出版社，2010.

[11] 广东民族学院中文系编. 黎族民间故事选［M］. 上海：上海文艺出版社，1983.

[12] 广东省海南黎族苗族自治州群众艺术馆. 黎族民间故事选［M］. 五指山：广东省海南黎族苗族自治州群众艺术馆，1981.

[13] 郭建中. 文化与翻译［M］. 北京：中国对外翻译出版公司，

2003：275.

［14］郭彧斌.奥康纳《西藏民间故事》英译本叙事建构探析［J］.西藏研究,2020（1）.

［15］韩伯泉.论黎族神话里的雷公［J］.学术论坛,1985（8）.

［16］胡庚申.翻译适应选择论［M］.武汉：湖北教育出版社,2004：125.

［17］黄晓坚.海南黎族传说研究［D］.北京：中央民族大学,2019.

［18］黄欣.当代黎族文学研究论析［D］.广州：广东技术师范学院,2014.

［19］金蕾.黎族非物质文化遗产黎锦传统文化研究［D］.青岛：青岛大学,2015.

［20］李淑媛.郭小东与黎族文学［D］.广州：广东技术师范学院,2015.

［21］刘唱,闫一亮,徐思鹏."文化翻译"观视域下的赫哲族民间故事外宣翻译［J］.文化创新比较研究,2020（4）.

［22］刘耀荃.海南岛古代历史的若干问题［J］.中南民族学院学报（社会科学版）,1986（S1）：108.

［23］龙敏,黄胜招.黎族民间故事集［M］.海口：南海出版公司,2002.

［24］茅盾.神话研究［M］.天津：百花文艺出版社,1981.

［25］彭玉斌.黎族民间童话教材选编［M］.北京：中国言实出版社,2013.

［26］曲明鑫.从黎族文化到黎族文学的历史变迁［J］.民族论坛,2015（5）.

［27］曲明鑫.黎族作家文学的民族性和开放性研究［D］.上海：华东师范大学,2008.

［28］曲明鑫.浅析黎族作家文学对黎族民间故事的借鉴［J］.时代文学,2012（3）.

[29] 曲明鑫，李默. 论黎族作家文学对黎族神话传说的继承［J］. 大众文艺，2011（9）.

[30] 石立坚. 专名与通名［J］. 语文建设，1987（3）.

[31] 史图博. 海南岛民族志［M］. 广州：中国科学院广东民族研究所，1964.

[32] 孙海兰，焦勇勤. 黎族民间文学的特点及保护［J］. 山东行政学院山东省经济管理干部学院学报，2006（3）.

[33] 孙有康，李和弟. 黎族创世史诗五指山传［M］. 广州：暨南大学出版社，1990.

[34] 孙致礼. 四十年的翻译历程：从跟潮到闯新路［C］//徐宏，等，主编. 寻找"原文的回声"：孙致礼翻译思想研讨会论文集. 武汉：武汉大学出版社，2019：5.

[35] 孙致礼. 文化与翻译［J］. 外语与外语教学，1999（11）.

[36] 王海. 艺术的发展与精神的传承：汉文化影响下的黎族民间文学［J］. 广东技术师范学院学报，2006（3）.

[37] 王海. 黎族文化研究著述概评［J］. 西南民族大学学报（人文社科版），2005（7）.

[38] 王海. 口传的历史"文本"：黎族民间文学概观［J］. 广东技术师范学院学报，2005（1）.

[39] 王海. 黎族民间长诗辨析［J］. 民族文学研究，2005（1）.

[40] 王海. 古远而丰厚的沉淀：试论几组黎族神话和神奇故事的文化意蕴［J］. 民俗研究，2005（2）.

[41] 魏怡. 国家非遗项目"耿村故事"的英译［J］. 石家庄铁道大学学报，2015（1）.

[42] 文明英，文京. 黎语长篇话语材料集［M］. 北京：中央民族大学出版社，2009.

[43] 向丽. 百年来国内外黎族研究述评［J］. 广西民族师范学院学报，2013（3）.

[44] 谢元. 海南黎族"兄弟"型民间故事研究［D］. 北京：中央

民族大学，2013.

［45］邢斌. 海南少数民族文学论析［J］. 琼州大学学报，2003（1）.

［46］邢植朝. 黎族文学总体观［J］. 民族文学研究，1988（4）.

［47］邢植朝. 黎族民间文学的发展与演变［J］. 海南师范学院学报，1989（3）.

［48］余杰. 海南黎族符号文化概观［J］. 民族论坛，2015（3）.

［49］苑中树. 黎族民间文学摭谈［J］. 中央民族大学学报，1995（6）.

［50］张睿. 海南黎族民歌文化研究［D］. 长春：东北师范大学，2016.

［51］周瑞婷. 文学生活中的族群想象［D］. 广州：广东技术师范学院，2017.